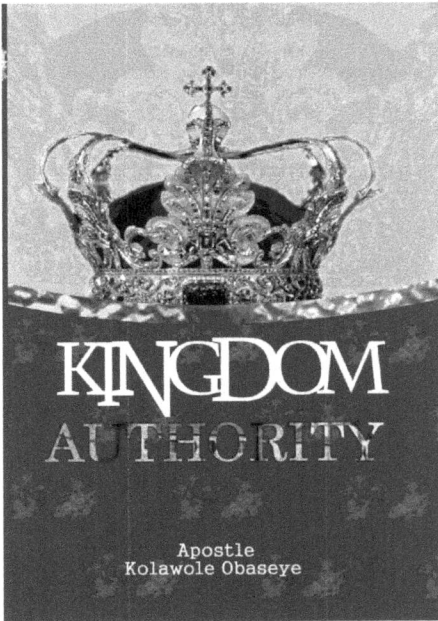

KINGDOM
AUTHORITY

Apostle
Kolawole Obaseye

KOLAWOLE OBASEYE
COPYRIGHT 2016

ISBN 978-978-086-079-0

Scriptural quotations are taken from the King James Version, the New King James Version and the Amplified Bible.
Published by
Kingsglory Publication
Kingsglory Avenue, Off Mukhtar Ramalan Yero Road
Gbagy Villa
Kaduna, Nigeria.

Contact: 08136891983, 08098243341.
Email- kingsgloryassembly@gmail.com

TABLE OF CONTENT

INTRODUCTION

God took the decision at a point in time to create His kind that will take charge of the affairs of heaven on earth. Hence, He formed man out of the dust of the earth and breathe into him His breath: His life and ability (Genesis 2:7). That gave man life and the mandate to be Lord and God on earth. It is that same breath in man that became the source of his relevance on earth; the means by which he is to exercise dominion. It was the same breath that was activated in Moses that made him a God over Egypt and her ruler (Pharaoh).

... the LORD said unto Moses, Take thee Joshua the son of Nun, a man in whom is the spirit, and lay thine hand upon him.
Numbers 27:18.

And Joshua the son of Nun was full of the spirit of wisdom; for Moses had laid his hands upon him.
Deuteronomy 34:9.

The ability of God was transferred to Joshua the son of Nun by Moses when he laid his hands upon him and that enabled him to bring the earth to a standstill. There is no limitation to that which the power of God can do. Therefore, do not limit yourself because you are the expression of God on earth.

Then spake Joshua to the LORD in the day when the LORD delivered up the Amorites before the children of Israel, and he said in the sight of Israel, Sun, stand thou still upon Gibeon; and thou, Moon, in the valley of Ajalon. And the sun stood still, and the moon stayed, until the people had avenged themselves upon their enemies.
Joshua 10:12-14.

Jesus, who is the Son of God and the Word made flesh, exerted the kingdom of God upon the earth even as a man because of the ability (breath) of God in Him.

And the spirit of the LORD shall rest upon him, the spirit of wisdom and understanding, the spirit of counsel and might, the spirit of knowledge and of the fear of the LORD.
Isaiah11:1, 2.

The Spirit of the Lord is upon me, because he hath anointed me to preach the gospel to the poor; he hath sent me to heal the brokenhearted, to preach deliverance to the captives, and recovering of sight to the blind, to set at liberty them that are bruised, To preach the acceptable year of the Lord.
Luke 4:18, 19.

The apostles of Jesus, by the same breath of God in them, turned the world upside down.

... But wait for the promise of the Father, which, saith he, ye have heard of me. But ye shall receive power, after that the Holy Ghost is come upon you: and ye shall be witnesses unto me both in Jerusalem, and in all Judea, and in Samaria, and unto the uttermost part of the earth ... These that have turned the world upside-down are come hither also.
Acts 1:4,8; 17:6.

The remarkable difference in the lives of these men was the Spirit of the Lord, the breath of the Almighty which was upon and in them. He is the Spirit of Lordship; the Spirit of authority; the force of the Seven Spirits of God by which He showed and will yet reveal to principalities and powers His manifold or multifaceted wisdom (Ephesians 3:10:Mark 6:2).

And the Lord shall send the ROD OF HIS STRENGTH out of Zion.
Psalm 110:2.

Kingdom authority is Heaven's mandate upon those who God has made rulers, kings and lords. Those who will rule, take charge over a domain and bring same, under the dominion of Jesus Christ who is Lord and King.

Thy kingdom come, thy will be done on earth as it is in Heaven.
Matthew 6:10.

Kingdom authority is the manifestation of the sevenfold dimensional power of God encapsulated in the Rod of His strength, which is the Holy Ghost, the power of the age to come. According to Prophet Daniel, no other kingdom will be stronger than the Kingdom of God. It will rule over every other kingdom

And in the days of these kings shall the God of heaven set up a kingdom, which shall never be destroyed: and the kingdom shall not be left to other people, but it shall break in pieces and consume all these kingdoms, and it shall stand for ever.
Daniel 2:44.

The kingdoms of this world are become the kingdoms of our Lord, and of his Christ; and he shall reign forever and ever.
Revelation 11:15.

That is why any believer who is conscious of this mandate destroys every work of darkness.

How God anointed Jesus of Nazareth with the Holy Ghost and with power: who went about doing good, and healing all that were oppressed of the devil; for God was with him.
Acts 10:38.

And these signs shall follow them that believe; in my name shall they cast out devils; they shall speak with new tongues; They shall take up serpents; and if they drink any deadly thing, it shall not hurt them; they shall lay hands on the sick, and they shall recover.
Mark 16: 17, 18.

This book was birthed in the place of revelation and to the intent that the consciousness of the mandate of heaven be created in the hearts of believers all over the world. Also, to build in us the confidence to take over the kingdoms of the earth, no matter how dark it is or becomes. Kingdom authority is what Christ gave to us His church, with a command, "occupy till I come." We are an army, God's battle axe, and His delegated authorities to earth. Discover the secret to occupying as you study this piece.

Apostle Kolawole Obaseye
(Senior Pastor, Kingsglory int'l Ministries)
January, 2016.

CHAPTER 1
KINGDOM AUTHORITY

And the Lord said unto Moses see, I have made thee a god to pharaoh...
Exodus 7:1.

Kingdom authority is heaven's mandate upon those God has made rulers, kings and lords. A good example of this is seen in the person of Moses. Moses ruled in the midst of his exactors and slave masters despite the immense pressure the children of Israel were under; the fortified army, large and strong. Upon God's mandate he reigned as a territorial principality regardless the person of pharaoh.

All that Moses needed was the Rod of strength out of Zion to rule in the midst of his enemies. It was not a product of educational expedience or his oratory proficiency although, he was well learned in all the wisdom of the Egyptians as revealed to us in Acts 7:22.
Kingdom authority means the mandate to rule, have charge over a domain and bring it under the domain of Jesus Christ.

The Rod Of Power

The Lord shall send the rod of thy strength out of Zion: Rule thou in the midst of thy enemies.
Psalm 110:2.

And the Lord said unto him, what is that in thine hand and he said a rod.
Exodus 4:2

.

And there shall come forth a rod out of the stem of Jesse and a branch shall grow out of his roots, the spirit of the Lord shall rest upon him, the spirit of wisdom and understanding, the spirit of counsel and might, the spirit of knowledge and of the fear of the Lord.
Isaiah 11: 1-2.

Upon that same rod is the spirit of dominion, the spirit of authority, which is the resultant force of the seven Spirits of God. Moses broke the strength of Pharaoh, the principality of Egypt via the activity of the seven Spirits of God.
Outstanding amongst the seven spirits was the spirit of wisdom by which Moses sponsored the deliverance of Israel. Scriptures tell us of the great things wisdom can do.

To the intent that now unto principalities and powers in heavenly places might be known by the church the manifold wisdom of God.
Ephesians 3:10 .

... and what wisdom is this which is given unto him, that even such mighty works are wrought by his hands?

Mark 6:2.

It is show time on earth. God through the church is going to legislate to principalities and powers a dimension of his many sided wisdom and rule in the midst of his enemies. There is a higher wisdom with which the church will discomfit the wisdom of the enemy. When the Bible says he will send the rod of his strength out of Zion to rule, it entails the seven fold dimension of the Spirit of God in power and authority.

When we talk about kingdom authority, we are talking about the seven fold dimension of power, being encapsulated in the rod which is the Holy Ghost. Reading down verse 4 of Isaiah 11, scripture tells us that; he shall rule with the rod of his mouth and judge the wicked with the breath of his lip. In the book of Revelation 19:15 it says, out of his mouth preceded a sword, a double edged sword, a rod by which he shall judge and destroy the wicked. So when scriptures says, he will give a mouth and a wisdom, it is basically referring to the rod of judgment as mentioned in Isaiah 11:4.

For I will give you a mouth and a wisdom which all your adversaries shall not be able to gainsay nor resist.
Luke 21:15.

... With the rod of his mouth and with the breath of his lips shall he slay the wicked.
Isaiah 11:4.

And out of his mouth goeth a sharp sword that he should smite the nation.
Revelation 19:15.

Jesus's breath upon his disciples was the seven fold dimension of the Holy Ghost. It was the rod with which the wicked would be destroyed. It was the mouth and wisdom which the adversary could not resist nor gainsay. What he gave them was the whole realities contained in the Holy Ghost, the custodian and the administrator of God's authority. So, when he breathed upon them, he gave them kingdom authority.

And when he said this, he breathed on them, and saith unto them, receive ye the Holy Ghost.
John 20:20.
Kingdom authority empowers you to subdue as the heroes of faith subdued kingdoms, quenched the mouth of lions and wrought righteousness. A generation is rising up who will walk in unequalled kingdom authority. I call them kingdom movers. They will carry and display such power that the whole kingdom of darkness cannot withstand.

Who through faith subdued kingdoms, wrought righteousness, obtained promises, stopped the mouths of lions, quenched the violence of fire, escaped the edge of the sword out of weakness were made strong, were valiant in fight turned to flight armies of the aliens. Women received their dead raised to life again...
Hebrews 11:33.

And saviours shall come up on mount Zion ...

Obadiah 1:21.

Scripture says out of Zion shall proceed saviours. For them to be saviours they must posses' kingdom strength to judge wickedness.

...the God of heaven set up a kingdom, which shall not be destroyed: and the kingdom shall not be left to other people, but it shall break in pieces and consume all these kingdoms, and it shall stand for ever.
Daniel 2:44.

God's eternal purpose will be executed through his kingdom addicts. According to Daniel 2:44, there is no other authority that will match the authority of this kingdom.

This kingdom will make other kingdoms varnish. That's why when you pray for sickness to leave, it goes because of the strength of the kingdom. The purpose of this book is to build kingdom confidence in you, so that it doesn't matter what darkness comes against you, you fear for nothing because nothing can bring down the kingdom of God.

Wherefore we receiving a kingdom which cannot be moved, let us have grace...
Hebrew 12:28.

A Delegated Authority

God is the supreme authority, He posses all authority and delegates it to his saints to fulfill heaven's mandate, with which he says "occupy till I come." You can't walk in true kingdom authority until you encounter him who is the supreme authority, because authority has its roots in God through the lord Jesus Christ. Every child of God has and can exercise a dimension of authority because of Jesus Christ. He has delegated authority to you to rule on earth. You are God's representative on earth and God has mandated you to go and occupy till he comes. You are his battle axe in these last days.

Thou art my battle axe and weapons of war: for with thee I will break in pieces the nation and with thee will I destroy kingdoms.
Jeremiah 51:20.

It was his authority but he gave it to you and that makes you a thousand times bigger on the inside than you are on the outside.

CHAPTER 2
THE KINGDOM

You did not only receive salvation when you became born again, you also received the kingdom. Jesus didn't only come to bring you salvation, but salvation is only a means through which the kingdom is introduced to you. Jesus death was the price of restoring kingdom back to man. The eternal purpose of God is the kingdom. God didn't give Adam salvation, he gave him kingdom, "be fruitful, multiply, rule, subdue."

...it is the father's good pleasure to give you the kingdom.
Luke 12:32.

Wherefore we receiving a kingdom which cannot be moved, let us have grace, whereby we may serve God acceptably with reverence and godly fear.
Hebrew 12:28.

Kingdom advancement is traceable to men who are equipped with authority in the realm of the spirit and with the understanding of the king's demand. Every failure to take back grounds the enemy has stolen, points to the fact that men of authority are not available. The expansion of the rule of God in any territory depends on men of authority, men in alignment with heaven, men whose presence is a threat to the kingdom of darkness because the know how to throw 'God's weight' around. The Bible says the kingdom of God is within you; this propels you to become conscious of what you carry and by such consciousness, rule in the midst of your enemies.

Men that walk in kingdom authority carry the character of Jesus, the lion of the tribe of Judea. The bible describes a righteous man as being bold as a lion because he has a right standing with God, which is the strength of walking in kingdom authority. Just like the lion, the righteous man fears nothing, and never turns back in the time of challenges. The greatest tool of the enemy is fear. He attempts to put fear in you, in order to cripple you. Stop seeing how big the enemy is, see the power and authority of God's kingdom and that kingdom is within you.

Kingdom Operates by Faith

Kingdom men are men of strong faith. Faith is a conviction, it is based on a knowing, a conviction stronger than what your physical eyes can see or what your hand can touch. It is the substance and reality of things you have not held; the assurance that you are going to have the things you desire. It is this conviction that makes a man go any length or pay any price when necessary, to walk in the full authority available for every child of God. Understanding is the bedrock of faith. When you understand the modus operandi and dynamics of God's kingdom, you move in His conquering strength, even in the midst of terrible oppositions. Satan attacks your faith in order to know how much understanding of this superior kingdom is embedded in your heart. When the enemy succeeds in putting fear in you, he has practically weakens God's ability in you which he dreads. This in turn, cripples your authority.

What Is Kingdom?

Kingdom is a sphere of dominion in which a king rules supreme.

It is a sphere of government where the will and authority of a king reigns supreme, and where he does everything within his power to protect the domain of his influence. The king is either a monarch or ruler who makes decrees and laws that protect the sphere of his influences.

Kingdom is the invisible government of God which is established upon our hearts.

Kingdom is the domain and dominion of a king.
In the center of every kingdom is a throne, when the throne of God becomes functional in our hearts then the influence of His authority will be felt among men. A throne also means that a government is present.

What is Government?

Government is a system that enforces laws and decrees that protect the sphere of influence of a king. When you talk about kingdom, you are also talking about its government. In every kingdom there is a government that enforces its decrees and rules.

When God made you a king, he gave you a government to enforce kingdom laws and decrees. So if anybody trespasses your area of jurisdiction, you have a government that enforces dominion over it. When the bible says he has made you a king and priest, it means he has placed within you the ability to rule. The parliament of heaven goes into action to enforce the rights and decrees of men by heaven's authority.

For where the word of a king is, there is power.
Ecclesiastes 8:4.

Jesus said to his disciples when you go to preach, say, the kingdom is at hand: the rule of God is at hand (activating kingdom authority by declaration). After that declaration, heal the sick and raise the dead. This is because, for God to restore the destiny of man, He needed to restore the

kingdom back to man. That's why, the model prayer of Jesus that his will be done on earth was preceded by "thy kingdom come", for it is only then can his will to heal, to save, and to deliver be done on earth, because in the kingdom lies everything man will ever need.

Kingdom Power and Glory

For thine is the kingdom, the power and the glory.
Matthew 6:13.

Once you have the kingdom of God, you are connected to the power and glory of God.

To whom also he shewed himself alive after his passion by many infallible proofs, being seen of them fourty days, and speaking of the things pertaining to the kingdom of God.
Acts 1:3.

The most important thing to the true believer is the kingdom of God. Remember, the kingdom of God is righteousness, peace and joy in the Holy ghost. The Holy Ghost is the communicator of the Kingdom of God. When the kingdom is established in you, the power of the Holy Ghost is available to you.

Power is the visible evidence of kingdom. Power is supernatural strength to change natural things. Power is a gift but authority is relationship based. Power can abide for a very long time but authority can be lost when you break relationship with God. Satan's disobedience made him to lose his authority but he however retained power with which he still deceives the world. Power is a proof that you were or are still connected to authority but authority is only functional because of positioning and alignment to God. kingdom authority is presence driven, it draws its strength from the 'person' of God. Both authority and power are measurable based on our walk and submission to God. Satan's greatest fear of the believer is not based on the power he possesses but his authority in God. Power can be manifested without authority but it won't stand the test of time.

The believer's authority is useless without the presence of God because it is sourced from a relationship with God, while power doesn't necessarily have to be about a relationship. This is the reason power works for a season. It is limited when it doesn't have authority: the presence of God as its continual source! When you are kingdom minded, you are backed up by the throne of God itself. The realm of the spirit recognizes that power is a by-product of kingdom authority and it is for confrontation while kingdom is for ownership and dominion. Kingdom empowers you with authority when you come under the dominion of the king and abide in the tutelage of the Holy Spirit who is the scepter of the king.

Authority makes you stand in the place of God and make decrees. A person of authority is able to do terrible things in righteousness because he is a prince of God, and has stature with God. He carries the name of God upon his forehead. He is of a special breed that stands out for God, a man through whom God will do great things.

The Kingdom of Heaven

Bible says for forty days after Jesus was raised, he went about manifesting infallible proofs and teaching things concerning the kingdom. This should be the lifestyle of every kingdom person. He spent those forty days so that you and I can understand how our lives should be ordered. Little wonder, the disciples manifested such great signs and wonders because no serious minded person stays under a practical lecture and finds it difficult to practice same.

Again, the kingdom of heaven is like unto a treasure hid in a field; the which when a man hath found, he hideth, and for joy thereof goeth and selleth all that he hath, and buyeth that field.

Matthew 13:44.

The kingdom of heaven is like a hidden treasure, it is not hid from the called but for the called and it belongs to the hungry, so that not all can access it, though it is actually available to all. When the man found it, he hid it in a field and did not just buy the treasure, but went and sold all that he had to buy the field.

All the labour of man is nothing compared to what the kingdom offers. If you invest your time in the kingdom, it will produce for you what no man can give to you. It means the toils of many years cannot be compared to the result of your labour in the kingdom.

The kingdom is so important, that Jesus spent the entire forty days after his resurrection teaching on it. Your greatness lies in the kingdom. Scripture says seek ye first the kingdom and every other thing will be added (Mathew 6:33). That which the world toils for, shall be added unto you. Upon this did Jesus teach his disciples how to transact kingdom in prayer; when you pray – "say thy kingdom come ..."

This is because the kingdom is most important. If you explore the kingdom, the world will look for you, you will be celebrated and be in the hallmark of history. The importance of this kingdom is the reason Paul said "I count all things but loss for the Excellency of the knowledge of Him (Philippians 3:8).

There are more things about the kingdom that the church has not broken into, it is yet to be fully explored. When Jesus told the young rich man to sell all he has and give to the poor, he was sorrowful because he did not understand the value of the kingdom. If he understood, he would have done it joyfully. This tells you that many believers carry the kingdom within them yet lack the understanding of its depth, strength and wealth. Until light comes, you will remain in darkness.

The kingdom of God is so special that the blessings available therein cannot be compared to what any man can give. Some people look for help from men. God is saying, you will be a marvel to your generation if you can discover and explore what is within you. So, it depends on the light and revelation you have about it. Your fears of the unknown will die at the revelation of the kingdom within you.The Kingdom of God is Righteousness, Peace & Joy.

For the kingdom of God is not meat and drink; but righteousness, and peace, and joy in the Holy Ghost.
Romans 14:17.

Righteousness

What is righteousness? Righteousness means to be in a state of vital being under God: where you are, and who you ought to be. Righteousness means to be as He is. It has very little to do with what you do, rather, what Jesus did. It means "as He is, so are we". It is an act of being right and not just an act of doing right, though, it also entails that. It is a state of being. It means to stand before God with no inferiority complex. It means to have statue with God. Bible says "... He is not ashamed to call them brethren."

For both he that sanctifieth and they who are sanctified are all of one: for which cause he is
not ashamed to call them brethren.
Hebrews 2:11.

That is why righteousness is a gift. When scripture says "the kingdom of God is righteousness..." it implies that the kingdom of God brings you into a state of being where you are not less equal with God.

When you understand kingdom, even the tips of your fingers will emit such power that is unequal with what the whole kingdom of darkness can do. When we teach righteousness, some people think we are making people bigger than what they are, but that is actually what it is. The bible refers to Jesus as the righteousness of God; he has become to us righteousness. He is our righteousness! We don't do anything to qualify for it, we are just in a state of being, a vital state of being. Righteousness makes you able to do things you couldn't have been able to do physically and things which spiritually, you couldn't have afforded or paid for.

Peace

Romans 14:17 says "the kingdom of God is peace..." What is peace? The word peace here means "EREN..." it is not Shalom, not the peace word for Shalom. It is a Greek word "ERENI" which means, a state of well being. These are three heavy words; righteousness-just like God, then it went further to say peace-which means a state of having everything; well being in every area of your life. And finally it says joy in the Holy Ghost.

When the kingdom of God comes upon you, it can change your state of being. The poverty will be gone and everything is yours, you are okay, needing no aid. Peace means absence from oppression and destruction. It also means a vital state of possessing everything, lacking nothing. This is what you have in the kingdom of God. No wonder it says repent for the kingdom is about to come, a realm you've never participated in. It is mind blowing! That is why you have to repent because your mind can never comprehend this truth. The bible says unless you receive it like a child, you can never enter into it. What does it mean? It is not being childish. It means being simple to the point you accept whatever you are taught as it is, even when your logical reasoning rejects it.Have you discovered that if you tell a child anything he easily accepts it?

Making the word of God of none effect through your tradition...
Matthew 7:13.

The bible says through your tradition, you have made the word of God of no effect. It may be too heavy for your mind, but take it as it is. That is the way you walk in the kingdom. When you come into it, you are going to walk in a different sphere of life. It will not be the way it used to be, hence you have to turn, repent from the way you think and think the way God thinks. The first message from Jesus was on the kingdom, and the lesson was that you have to repent to enter into the kingdom of God.

The bible says it will be easier for a camel to enter into the kingdom of God than it will be for the rich man. Why? The rich man got his riches through his calculative means. A camel, however, is a moron. It just follows. Though bigger in size than its owner, it submits to the mind of the owner. That is why it is easier for it to enter. A rich man will question how? That was why when Jesus asked the rich young ruler to go and sell everything he had, he couldn't do it because he did not understand it. The kingdom is not what you enter by what you have achieved, rather, you enter empty to achieve what you desire because provisions have already been made available for you there. The bible says, flesh and blood shall not inherit the kingdom of God. Whatever you amass in your ability cannot be part of the kingdom. No matter how much you try to convince people to believe that your wealth is for the kingdom, when it is not, God will prove it. He is the one that prospers you through His grace. The kingdom realm is just different.

Joy In the Holy Ghost

Romans 14:17 further states that, "the kingdom of God is ...joy in the Holy Ghost". It means the righteousness, peace, and joy are all in the Holy Ghost. So the kingdom of God is actually in the Holy Ghost. The joy of the Lord is your strength because joy is in the kingdom, and the bible says "seek ye first the kingdom of God and His righteousness and everything shall be added." So everything is in the kingdom, just seek and everything will be added. You don't work for it, you yield yourself to it. Scripture says "with joy shall you draw from the well of salvation." Salvation is in the kingdom and with it you draw from the kingdom. That is why joy is not a fruit of accomplishment but a fruit of the spirit. It is only produced in the spirit, hence you must be born again to participate in it.

But the fruit of the Spirit is love, joy, peace, longsuffering, gentleness, goodness, faith, meekness, temperance: against such there is no law.
Galatians 5:22-23.

It is a fruit of your recreated spirit because the Holy Ghost resides in your spirit; it is a nature. All the fruit of the spirit are the nature of the Holy Spirit and because He resides in you, your spirit takes the same nature. When you became born again, your spirit was recreated, as such, the Holy Ghost lives in you and he enables you to manifest His joy.

But before you can fetch from the kingdom, you must first have the righteousness of Christ. You must have that statue that makes you act God wherever you go. You also need to have the peace of God which supplies all your need. So when I declare 'Kingdom,' I am not wishing God will answer. I know that because of the righteousness I have, I am acting God, and because of the peace I have, I possess everything, lacking nothing. So, based on what I posses and where I am, when I declare 'Kingdom,' I bring healing to your body by his grace. When you preach Kingdom, you are not trying to raise small 'Jesus' who will be replaced with a bigger 'Jesus' when he fails. The bible says "ye are Christ". When you preach kingdom, you manifest Christ. "As the Father has sent me, so send I you". You are not less than He is. That is also why you have the same Holy Ghost with the one in Jesus.

Herein is our love made perfect, that we may have boldness in the day of judgment: because as he is, so are we in this world.
1 John 4:17.

The bible says "... as He is, so are we in this world". It says all the fullness of God bodily is in Jesus Christ, and of that fullness have we received. The moment we accepted Jesus we received the kingdom, we became reconfigured with a recreated spirit. Kingdom teaching enables us to understand that everything that is in God has been diffused into us. That is why it says "the kingdom of God is within you". Everything you need in life, be it provisions or ability to accomplish your destiny, are all in the kingdom. However, we can only enjoy the realities of this provision by declaring them.

When we speak them, they materialize, "and the word becomes flesh" (John1:14). So cars, children, marriages, money, are all in dematerialized form in the spirit. We carry a load of provisions but since it is the Holy Ghost who is actually carrying them, they are so light. So when you say, I can make you rich, people should believe you and not wonder what you have. What I carry, the whole banks in the world can't contain it but because of the realm I'm operating in, it's all dematerialized and kept in the Spirit. How do you think the world was formed? ...from things which do not appear... how can things come from things which do not appear...? They come from a Spirit realm. The bible said He sent forth His Spirit and the world was made.

The entire creation was in the Spirit, which is why God can be everywhere at the same time, being a Spirit. All material blessings are in the Holy Ghost and He in turn kept it in you. But before you can 'materialize them, you need joy, hence scripture says with joy you shall draw from the well of salvation. It is so simple that no matter the kind of bad news you hear, it is not the final say. Until you say it is over, it is not.

Joy Everlasting

> *A merry heart doeth good like a medicine: but a broken spirit drieth the bones.*
> *Proverbs 17:22.*

> *My brethren, count it all joy when ye fall into divers temptations.*
> *James 1:2.*

So when I see a bad situation, I rejoice, not because of what has happened but for the change about to take place. The bible says in all things rejoice. Why rejoicing? For the kingdom will be made manifest. Once your spirit is broken, you are defeated, but if your spirit remains high, you can draw from the well of salvation. So with joy, you draw from the well of salvation. It is that strength from which you draw that you will bring salvation and deliverance to the people.

David said "he gives me a song in the night season". When everything is down, there's one thing you must not lose, a song. If you've lost your song, you've lost your breakthrough. People who are very sensitive know that the darkest hour is the hour before dawn, so when they are supposed to be crying, they begin to dance. Can you imagine laughing and rejoicing when things are bad? Are you mad? Yes, in the Holy Ghost. Let's learn to draw joy from the well of our salvation through the Holy Ghost which is not dependent on any musical instrument, but on the finished works of Christ.

CHAPTER 3
KINGDOM REALITIES

T he proof and uniqueness of any kingdom is in the realities that exist within it. Otherwise, it is like any other kingdom. How do you know that a kingdom is special? You know it by the distinctive realities that exist in it.

Even as they delivered them unto us, which from the beginning were eyewitnesses, and ministers of the word; it seem good also, having had perfect understanding of all things from the very first…
Luke 1:2-4.

The former treatise have I made, O Theophilus, of all that Jesus began both to do and teach.
Acts 1:1.

A letter from an eyewitness with perfect understanding of the earlier operations and impact of the kingdom, writes to Theophilus to keep him abreast with kingdom realities, in order for him to know the expectations on him "… that thou mightiest know the certainty of those things, wherein thou has been instructed". What was the instruction? "… of the former treaties which Jesus began to do and to teach". The Letter is to the same person at different times, as a way of remembrance and a follow up to the first letter. In the first letter, he said "I write to you that you may know the order of things", so that you can come to that perfect understanding with me. In the second letter, he tells him of the understanding he wants him to come into; "of the things which Jesus did and taught". The things which he did and taught are invitations to us to walk in the realm of his realities. Scripture says they are written for our examples.

Citizens Of The Kingdom

Heaven is not a natural place or geographical location; it is a realm and dimension we live in by the spirit. It is a realm! Bible says your citizenship is in heaven (Philippians 3:20). We don't die to go to heaven, we are already in heaven by reason of our being in Christ. You operate in that realm by the spirit. That means whatever is done in heaven can also be done on earth while we still live in the flesh.

You may choose to die before partaking of heavenly realities such as the fire on the throne, angels, precious stones and other supernatural realities around the throneroom. But you must know that Heaven is not only entered into by death but through the spirit. Though, the seemingly easiest way to enter heaven is through physical death which frees your spirit from bodily limitation, it doesn't always have to be so. If you understand that it is by the spirit, you will not have to wait to die to experience the things in heaven.

And no man hath ascended up to heaven, but he that came down from heaven, even the Son of man which is in heaven.
John 3:13.

Jesus said that he was in heaven while on earth, because he understood that it was the yielding of his spirit and the help of the Holy Ghost that aided his operation in heaven while he was on earth. Many of you are limited to only earthly experiences because you have not been taught to live in heaven by the spirit while you are still on earth. The world has educated only your human senses, and that has become your limitation. We have been taught of only what our physical eyes can see, what our ears can hear and what our bodies can feel. There are certain realities that belong to us but we cannot access them without building a kingdom mindset /consciousness; that we are citizens of the kingdom of heaven.

The realities you don't interface with you can't experience and what you cant experience you cant represent. When Jesus told Nicodemus that he saw him under the sycamore tree, he was shocked, unknown to him, there is no barricade in the realm of the spirit. God doesn't call anything supernatural, because in His world, what you call supernatural is natural. Therefore, we can begin to operate in those dimensions of heaven while on earth naturally. God is saying to his church, it is time to operate in the supernatural, naturally, because it truly belongs to us. The supernatural should be our lifestyle.

The eyes of your understanding being enlightened; that ye may know what is the hope of his calling, and what the riches of the glory of his inheritance in the saints.
Ephesians 1:18.

It is not a promotion whenever a believer engages in supernatural activities or starts performing miracles. If I raise the dead, it's not a promotion, because in heaven, there is nothing called death. What happens when I raise the dead is that I came to the realization and activation of the realities in the realm where I belong. So it's natural in the realm of heaven that things don't die, but my lack of understanding can be a limitation and I won't be able to do anything when I lose consciousness of my stand in that realm.

To me, the prayer of Paul in Ephesians is the greatest prayer ever prayed. If you don't know what to pray, pray Ephesians 1:18-21. After Jesus came, the heavens have been perpetually opened for us to participate in. What we need is understanding of its operation.

For with thee is the fountain of life: in thy light shall we see light.
Psalm 36:9.

Remember Heaven is the realm you live in by the spirit. It is important for you to live in this consciousness and keep pursuing every reality available in heaven until you experience them. That's why Paul prayed to be apprehended of that for which also he was apprehended of. (Philippians 3:10). it is in knowing him that we partake in these realities.

The bible tells us that in his light, we find light; light means revelation. It is from the revelation of the king that we find the revelation of ourselves and what has been made available to us. Jesus is the syllabus of our existence, so that anything we see in him becomes the things that are functional in us. Every promise you see in the bible is available for all believers who will break into it by hunger and revelation. Hunger leads you to search for what you know has been made available for you. It is kept not from you, but for you.

A Kingdom Of Infallible Proofs

Until the day he was taken up, after that he through the Holy Ghost had given commandments unto the apostles whom he had chosen. To whom also he shewed himself... by many infallible proofs ... And speaking of the things pertaining the kingdom
Acts 1:2-3.

Infallible proofs means undeniable proofs. It entails miracles, signs and wonders as evidences of the kingdom. The kingdom of God is evident when these realities manifest. That is the reason this chapter is titled kingdom realities, which should become a common place in our life.

And heal the sick that are therein, and say unto them, the kingdom of God is come nigh unto you.
Luke 10:9.

To many, Christianity has lost its power and has become a mere religion because it has been reduced to mere words. The Bible calls it "having the form of godliness but denying the power thereof". They have a form but lack the power to show it forth. It has been reduced to a form. As said earlier, Heaven is not a place but a realm we live in by the spirit. You may go to heaven when you die, but you can as well live there now by your spirit. True kingdom teaching says you can also operate heaven on earth by your spirit. The flesh or distance is not a barrier or a problem in operating heaven's realities.

For our citizenship is in heaven...
Philippians 3:20.

By the reason of being saved you have been brought in to sit in a new place, as citizens of heaven. When you see a man manifest supernatural dimension, it is not because he is special or better than others rather, it is the understanding of where he is seated in the heavenly and his level of being surrendered to God. You, as well as the people around you will be shocked at what God will do with you if you yield yourself to the Holy Ghost. Just like a baby in the womb of its mother has potential within him, he does not need to cry or stretch part of its body, to grow ears, mouth, eyes, etc but as he feeds, those features develop and function properly. This is the same with the believer. As he feeds and exercise his spiritual senses, he will be able to function well in the realm of the spirit. Kingdom realities will take a common place, even kids will begin to manifest some dimensions.

But strong meat belongeth to them that of full age even those who by reason of use have their senses exercised to discern both good and evil.
Hebrews 5:14

I have made up my mind to break into all the realities that are available to me. I have made up my mind not to live in the shadow of any man of God, not for competition but because it is available to all and scripture admonishes us to covet spiritual gifts.

A man went to Israel and met a group of Rabbis, who don't believe in Jesus as the Savior of the world. In a bid to prove who Jesus was, the man asked if anyone had a leg shorter than the other and they pointed at one. He prayed for him in the name of Jesus and his shorter leg grew out, the Rabbis were amazed and one of them accepted the lordship of Jesus. He was converted immediately and went about with the same excitement growing out people's legs with similar disparity, until he grew out forty legs within a short period of time.

You see, it is available and you can experience the realities of heaven. The disciples of Jesus Christ according to history were young but they shook nations because they understood kingdom and operated in its realities.

Realities Of Eternal Value

The Lord hath prepared his throne in the heavens; and his kingdom ruleth over all.
Psalm 103:19.

Every reality in the kingdom is of eternal value. That is why the bread of heaven sustained Elijah for forty days. The Israelites travelled under the influence of this kingdom for forty years with their clothes growing with them. Things that seem impossible are made possible in the kingdom. The power available in this kingdom beats any medical achievement, such that at a mere declaration of a word, cancer melts away. These are the realities available in the kingdom. So much was that reality that manna was provided from heaven.

They were asked not to keep any beyond each day for five days and twice as much on the sixth for the sixth and the seventh day which was the Sabbath day. Those who disobeyed had their manna turned into maggots. It was not like they have been eating maggot all the while but once the kingdom life is removed from anything, it takes a natural form. That means you can take away nature by bringing in the kingdom. The teaching on kingdom is not effective if its reality is not evident in your life.

And in the days of these kings shall the God of heaven set up a kingdom, which shall never be destroyed: and the kingdom shall not be left to other people, but it shall break in pieces and consume all these kingdoms, and it shall stand for ever.
Daniel 2:44.

Psalm 103:19 and Daniel 2:44 tells you that the kingdom of God shall swallow up all other kingdoms because it is superior. Scripture says He rules with the rod of his strength. This means, you are given the mandate to rule. Stop seeing the kingdom as a location. It is a realm, and the scripture says that realm is in you, it is locked up in your inside.

Seeing And Receiving The Kingdom

1.   Be Born Again

Notwithstanding in this rejoice not, that the spirits are subject unto you; but rejoice because your names are written in heaven ...
Luke 10:20.

They were rejoicing that demons were answerable to them. But Jesus told them not to rejoice that the devils were obedient to them but to rejoice more, that their names were written in heaven, not in the book of life. It means that your name is registered in the kingdom of heaven where you rule. Once your name is written there, you are lord over everything under heaven.

> *He that cometh from above is above all.*
> *John 3:31.*

Great things are available in the kingdom. That is why Jesus told Nathaniel not to be amazed at the things he had heard but to wait until he sees Angels ascending and descending upon the son of man. This means there are greater realities to come.

> *Jesus answered and said unto him, Verily, verily, I say unto thee, except a man be born again,*
> *he cannot see the kingdom of God.*
> *John 3:3.*

Some realites of the kingdom of God can be seen, and it is being born again that qualifies a man to see or enter into the kingdom. When you became born again, you were qualified to be taught kingdom realities.This kingdom as said earlier is a sphere of government, a sphere of dominion which gives a person, a king or a monarch absolute power to take the decisions he needs to take in order to protect his domain and a government is a system that enables you enforce authority. In every government, there is a seat of power. That seat of power is what the Bible refers to as throne. (Hebrews 12:22).

Your inception into the kingdom starts with repentance; "repent for the kingdom of God." You enter into the kingdom by turning away from the way you think and do things, by changing your perspective and taking God's order of doing things. This launches you into the kingdom. John in the book of revelation said, "He was in the spirit", and he heard a voice calling him to come up! When he turned, suddenly, he was in the throne room. Being born again is not a will not to commit sin, it means to be turned into another realm, the kingdom realm. When you become born again, the ability to commit sin loses its effect on you because you have 'turned' and have taken up a new identity which is God's nature that delivers you from the nature of sin, and imparts into you power from the throne of God. The Bible says "As many as received him he gave them power to become", so when you receive him, the ability to live right comes upon you.

Throneroom Realities

> *And above the firmament that was over their heads was the likeness of a throne, as the*
> *appearance of a sapphire stone: and upon the likeness of the throne was the likeness as the*
> *appearance of a man above upon it.*
> *Ezekiel 1:26.*

Ezekiel in a vision saw a whirlwind, out of which proceeded fire and out of the fire proceeded the four living creatures and out of that came a wheel, like a wheel within a wheel out of which proceeded a throne. The activities around the throne are so powerful, and on that throne sat, the most powerful.

> ... *but ye are come unto mount Zion, unto the city of the living God...Unto Jesus...Unto an innumerable company of angels...unto the judge of all.*
> *Hebrew 12:22-23*

Mount Zion is where God dwells; mount Zion is the kingdom of God. Heaven is His throne and the earth His footstool. The city of God is mount Zion. God lives in Mount Zion, Which is a dimension in eternity; it is an eternity realm where God dwells.

God has a city, the heavenly Jerusalem with an innumerable company of angels. Revelation 18:1 tells us of an angel whose glory covered the entire earth and another in Revelation 19:17 that can stand in the sun and cover the brightness of the sun. If angels who are servants can do these, then how big and vast is God. Angels can be super big. Before you see an angel you must be in a vision, so you see them in a sizeable form; the way God sees them.

> *To the general assembly and the church (i.e. there is an assembly and then the church) of the first born who are registered in Heaven, to God the judge of all on of the things you came into when you became born again is the judge of all, when you came into the city of God.*
> *Hebrews 12: 23*

The Bible says we have fellowship and the fellowship is with the father (1 John 1:3). You came into this union when you became born again.
Being born again means to be regenerated into the kingdom life. When you truly become born again, the dimension of the higher life super imposes itself on the dimension of the lower life you have been living in. Living a righteous life is only possible with the kingdom life.

2.   Spiritual Hunger

Make up your mind that you will not just read about these realities in scripture and it ends there but that you will experience them. I insist on the experiences available in the kingdom, so I keep pressing.

> *Blessed are they which do hunger and thirst after righteousness: for they shall be filled.*
> *Matthew 5:6.*

People who are not hungry, seldom find what they are not looking for. Hunger is the key to access the realities in the kingdom. The Bible says "blessed are they who hunger and thirst after righteousness, for they shall be filled (Mathew 5:6)". That righteousness is not just the righteousness of being free from sin. It also entails having the ability to stand in God's capacity. But you must hunger for this righteousness. Countless realities are available in the kingdom but are only accessible by hunger. You can grow into a reality with the ability to judge the tribes of the earth (Luke 22:30). As you press in, more realities are made accessible to you.

Through your hunger, you can access certain depths and realities in the kingdom. The greatest limitation is not the absence of realities but the absence of hunger to access it. You can fetch these realities if only you are hungry.

Through desire a man having separated himself, seeketh and intermeddleth with all wisdom.
Proverb 18:1.

...since that time the kingdom of God is preached and every man presseth into it.
Luke 16:16.

I love it when I read that Ezekiel was caught up by the locks of his head. What a realm! I love when I saw where Jesus told the disciples to go and pick a coin from the mouth of a fish. These miracles show you that indeed location is not a problem once you understand how the kingdom functions.

Ask me, and I shall give thee the heathen for thine inheritance, and the uttermost part of the earth for thy possession.
Psalm 2:8.

When we have those realities manifested on earth, people will begin to respect our gospel. I have seen strange miracles take place when we press in hunger.

3.   Stay Conscious

The king of this kingdom is the governor of all governors. His kingdom rules above every other and scripture says that kingdom is in you. That means, you are carrying the governor of all governors (Psalm 22:28). Daniel says he rules over the kingdom of men. It means that anywhere you find yourself whether in the physical or spiritual realm, you can rule. Stay conscious of the truth that the kingdom of God rules above all other kingdoms. It will help you overthrow every form of evil wherever you find yourself. You are the solution of mankind. You are a ruler on earth. Thus, wherever you find yourself and there is a challenge, don't ask what shall we do?", but tell them the solution has come. You must live with the consciousness that you are the answer of creation and that you are untouchable and unstoppable.

No one can touch you because you carry kingdom fire. The Bible says who can carry fire in his bosom and not be burnt? Whoever calls your name for evil, kingdom fire answers them. What you need is the consciousness of this reality. Scripture says faith comes by hearing and hearing by the word of God. So, submit yourself to hearing it. What is affecting our faith is the things we have been taught in the past. You need to 'renew' your mind, so that you can exert your kingdom power where needful. The word renew means to be brain washed; you let go your mind and get another. No wonder, the Bible admonishes us to let the mind of Christ be in us.

To have the mind of Christ means to have an anointed mind. It is a mind that thinks God's thought; a mind of dominion; a mind in charge; a conquering mind. If you have that mentality, nothing can harm you but if fear takes hold of you, the enemy has a chance of executing his plans against you. Christianity is reduced to mere religion if you don't have reality backing it up.

A Christian should be known by infallible proofs. Insist on manifesting these realities. There are realms and realities available for you. Don't live in the shadows of who you really are. Explore the dimensions in this kingdom, so that you can live in the fullness of the life you have in Christ.

CHAPTER 4
GOD'S PURPOSE FOR KINGDOM

Dispense Himself Into Man

T he will of God is that he may dispense himself into you, so that he constitutes his personality in your inner man. The purpose is that his flawless character, grace and power can find expression in the face of the earth through human vessels, so that they can walk the face of the earth like he walked before.

One of the reasons we study kingdom is that it may manifest and reign through us. God intends to rule the earth, which is why even when Adam failed, his purpose has not changed: though plans were altered, purpose remained.

"Now therefore, if ye will obey my voice indeed, and keep my covenant, then ye shall be a peculiar treasure unto me above all people: for all the earth is mine: and ye shall be unto me a kingdom of priests, and an holy nation..."
Exodus 19:5-6.

God's desire is to make you, a peculiar treasure, a kingdom of priest above all the people. Above all! The Bible says he has not called the sons of Jacob to seek Him in vain. He wants to make you a treasure; he wants to make you a display of who he is. The wealth of a man is often displayed through his children and other people around him.

When the Queen of Sheba saw just the garment of Solomon's servants, she fainted because it tells of his splendor. God wants to make you a peculiar treasure. If you walk with him, he will showcase Himself by the manifestation of his realities through you, which is the signatory of his glory on his saints. God wants to put a stamp of his personality on you. God constitutes himself in us by the strength of his throne upon our hearts, which is the throne of his government. The Bible says we are the temple of the Holy Ghost; our inner man is configured in such a way that we have become carriers of His dimensions. We are now vessels of his glory through which he can display His glory on the face of the earth.

When God created Adam, He created a physical type of himself that could be held and felt. You may say, God who is an all-powerful being is a spirit, so how can God be tangible? The mind can't fathom this. God's divine formula was that he poured himself into his son. He poured himself into his son Jesus Christ. Jesus on earth was the extension of God.

1Timothy 3:16
And without controversy great is the mystery of Godliness: God made manifest in the flesh, justified in the spirit, seen of angels...

The Son was God amongst us but God's ultimate dream was to live in man. In pursuit of God's dream, Jesus died to reconcile man to God, thereby transmitting the God life to anyone who receives him. 2 Corinthians 3:17 says, "...the Lord is that Spirit..." God now lives in us, in the person of the Holy Spirit. God is a Spirit (John 4:24), the Lord Jesus Christ is that Spirit (2 Corinthians 3:17) that now dwells in us as the Holy Ghost.

You must understand according to scripture, that the kingdom does not come by observation, it is not what you observe by your human senses, but what you know and have. As you read through this book, you should have an unshakeable confidence in what you carry inside of you. Though dangerous yet humble; lions yet sheep by the virtue of the nature of God in us – Humility is not fear, rather it is strength brought under control. What you carry is bigger than whatever threat that comes against your life.

You carry eternity inside of you. The Bible says "... eternity is in your heart (Ecclesiastes 3:11 HNV)". Eternity is not of the physical world; Eternity is a realm that is not within the scope of time. It is a timeless dimension. It is not bound by time, space and matter.

Time is a by-product of eternity. Eternity is in the Holy Ghost and the Holy Ghost resides in you. If you understand what you received when the Holy Ghost came inside of you, you won't be timid. Smith Wigglesworth said "I'm a thousand times bigger on the inside than I am on the outside".

Re-Colonising The Kingdoms Of The Earth

King Nebuchadnezzar, king of Babylon had a dream and in it he saw a statue with a head of fine gold, the arms of silver, the belly and thighs of brass, the legs of iron, and the feet a mixture of clay and iron.

... For as much as thou sawest that the stone was cut out of the mountain without hands, and that it brake in pieces the iron, the brass, the clay, the silver, and the gold; the great God hath made known to the king what shall come to pass hereafter: and the dream is certain, and the interpretation thereof sure.
Daniel 2:37-45.

The statue he saw was a representation of kingdoms: represented in gold was great Babylon; silver was the kingdom of the Medes and Persia; the third kingdom was the kingdom of the Greece which was the brass, after the Greece the Roman Empire was represented as clay and iron. The statue represented four Empires that have ruled the world.

Scriptures mention a stone coming from nowhere, hitting the statue at its feet and crushed it entirely. That stone was referred to as God's greater kingdom; greater than all the previous kingdoms put together. And that greater kingdom of God is within you, which means wherever you go everything will submit to the authority of God's government within you. It also means that wherever you enter, irrespective of how strong the powers there are, they will acknowledge that something greater has entered. If you carry this government, you don't fear.

And in the days of these kings shall the God of heaven set up a kingdom which shall never be destroyed: and the kingdom shall not be left to another people, but it shall break in pieces and consume all these kingdoms, and it shall stand for ever.
Daniel 2:44.

The church is that stone that will come upon every other demonic spiritual government. And every other government no matter how strong will come crumbling because of the government that works with you. The Bible speaking in Isaiah concerning Jesus said "the government would be upon his shoulder". Remember, Jesus Christ is the head of the church and we are the body where the shoulder is, so it is the church that is carrying that government of God that will crush the kingdom of Satan.

Matthew 16:18.
And upon this rock I will build my church; and the gates of hell shall not prevail against it.

To Do His Will On Earth

Thy kingdom come. Thy will be done in earth, as it is in heaven.
Matthew 6:10.

God wants the church to walk in the strength of his Government. The kingdom model Prayer starts with: Our father which art in heaven. Bear in mind that "Heaven is his throne". Then the prayer goes on "Hallowed be your name", what name? Isaiah tells us that his name shall be called "Wonderful, Counselor, and mighty God." Names give identity, nature and capacity to things... the expression "Hallowed be your name" also implies hallowed be the wonder, power and strength that comes from the dimension of his throne. It speaks of a reverence of the magnificence of the realities of the Wonderful, mighty God, miraculous one and Prince of Peace, and all these proceed from the throne where he sits in heaven.

"Thy kingdom come" implies that all his attribute as mentioned above come upon the earth. Bring down the spectrum of God's government on earth. Why? So that His will be done on earth as it is done in heaven. What is his will? To see the earth restored to heavenly patterns; where Jesus reigns supreme over evil via the seven Spirits of God; the spirit of the Lord, wisdom, knowledge, understanding, counsel, might, and of the fear of God.
The bible refers to them as the seven horns and fire proceeding out of the throne. The Lord's Prayer is therefore, a declaration of heaven on earth. SO THAT THE FULL ADMINISTRATION OF HIS GOVERNMENT BE SEEN ON EARTH.

For the kingdom is the Lord's: and he is the governor among the nations.
Psalms 22:28.

Now the Bible says "we've been translated from the power of darkness into the kingdom of God" (Colossian 1:13). Kingdom here talks about the power and ability of God. You can't separate kingdom from power. When you have the kingdom of God, you manifest his reality through your life, as such you become a tributary of his majestic power.

Of the increase of his government and peace there shall be no end, upon the throne of David, and upon his kingdom, to order it, and to establish it with judgment and with justice from henceforth even for ever. The zeal of the Lord of hosts will perform this.
Isaiah 9:7.

The church has the mandate to transform the earth with the resources of heaven. At the revelation of kingdom authority the church will be mantled with an unbeatable force. It will showcase the realities around the throne of God.

The true identity of the church is about to be seen. The sleeping giant will rise again and take its place in administrating the counsel of God upon the earth:

The ambassadorial assignment of the church will come to limelight. It will be by heaven's governmental anointing to rule the ground where wickedness had swayed. It will administrate the realm of the kingdom of God on the earth such that earth will become a perfect reflection of heaven. "… on earth as it is in heaven."

Kingdom, Not Democracy

Kingdom structure is not of democratic setting. Democracy brings one to a seat of power by the will of the people, and everything he does is controlled by the desire of the people and their expectations. The people determine what is done in democracy, Kingdom isn't so. Kingdom is a realm or sphere of dominion where the authority of a king reigns supreme. Where ever you find Kingdom, it is only the will and authority of the king that counts. Kingdom has to do with the will, authority and the power of a king. Kingdom is the domain and dominion of a king, it empowers the monarch or king with absolute power to make decisions or take actions he deems fit in order to protect or administer his will over a territory.

The judgment of a king is final and unquestionable. In kingdom, the will of the subject doesn't count. The king's will is supreme and non-contestable as long as you are within the jurisdiction of His domain. His will and words are laws which must be submitted to. Within the sphere of his influence, everything belongs to him. However God's kingdom is not anti people but against the wickedness from the kingdom of darkness; for God's nature is the nature of goodness and mercy

Where the word of a king is, there is power...
Ecclesiastes 8:4.

Kingdom Is Territorial

It was a contest of kingdoms when Satan took Jesus to the top of the pinnacle and said "all the kingdoms of this world I will give you", but the Bible already established about Jesus that "of the increase of his kingdom there shall be no end" (Isaiah 9:7). The Kingdoms of this world will become the kingdom of our God and of His Christ. Meaning, the kingdom of Christ in you has an increasing nature and every other kingdom is subject to it.

The church is the medium through which the kingdom of God will increase and every other kingdom will be subjected to it. Our being in Christ is so we could be vessels through which God's kingdom will increase. Any time the church comes under oppression, something has gone wrong, the understanding of kingdom isn't in place (Daniel 7:9). People suffer in life because they don't understand where they are seated in Christ. When the evidence of Christ's death isn't manifest in your life, it means another throne is in charge of your life. Hence, there is need for warfare against those thrones, however you must first empower your mind about who you are in Christ. You must speak from a place of authority and knock every other throne out. We do not fight from defeat to victory but from victory to victory because we have the proper perspective of our place in Christ, and when we speak, we are actually executing the mind of Christ.

Kings And Priests

And hast made us unto our God kings and priests: and we shall reign on the earth.
Revelation 5:10.

He has made us kings and Priests and we shall reign on earth, with that understanding, once we make decrees they are done, with no contention. Without the understanding of kingdom, you can't have victory over demonic manipulations as you should.

When Balaam said of the children of Israel "the shout of a king is in their midst" it means that as a king, whatever you say is a shout in the realm of the spirit. The Bible says "where the word of a king is, there is power." When you pray, you must have the mentality of a king that there can be no contention within the sphere of your rule. Demons are permitted to stay comfortably within the territories of them who do not know where they are seated. If evil prevails around you, it implies that you are not standing in your office as king. Christ has given you power over the works of the enemy and said nothing should by any means hurt you, for you are a king. God will not act on any matter upon the face of the earth because he has placed representatives and has mandated them to represent him. He has said whatever you bind on earth is bound in heaven and what you loose on earth is loosed in heaven (Matthew 18:18).

Submit yourselves therefore to God. Resist the devil, and he will flee from you.
James 4:7.

Whatever you allow in your life is what will happen, because you are a king. Authority is the order of kingdom. Whenever you speak, heaven will respond or act. He said "command ye me concerning the works of my hands" (Isaiah 45:11). But the secret is still traced to first being wholly submitted to the Lordship of the Lord Jesus Christ. The centurion in Matthew 8:9 understood the principle by which kingdom works, for he was a man under authority. A man not under authority cannot give authority. Scripture says submit yourself to the Lord, resist the devil and he will flee from you (James 4:7). If you don't submit yourself, you can't resist the devil. When the devil is not submitted to you, it is an indication that you have not been submitted to the Lord Jesus. You therefore, can't enjoy the power of the kingdom when you don't respect structure in the kingdom.

You can't rebuke when you are not under God's control. Jesus didn't come to bring salvation, he came to bring kingdom, and salvation was only an access to the kingdom. God gave Adam kingdom not salvation at the Garden of Eden. Kingdom is God giving you lordship and authority to rule on His behalf on earth. The present church today is only basking in salvation, but God wants us to function in kingdom, in the realm far above principalities and powers.

CHAPTER 5
THE REVELATION OF JESUS

In the beginning was the Word, and the Word was with God, and the Word was God.
John 1:1.

People can't understand the concept of the kingdom when it is done outside the revelation of Jesus. It must be done from the perspective of Jesus. The revelation of Jesus is not to make you an eloquent theologian, but that God may find expression through a people. By the revelation of Jesus, who is the word of God; God constitutes himself in you. The bible says "in the beginning was the word, and the word was with God..." (John 1:1). So, through his word, he constitutes his personality, nature, dominion, and grace into you.The word of God is also the seed that will bring about the delivery of God's promises to you. You carry the capacity for a miracle when you are full of expectation born from the word; your expectation is a womb in the spirit. Just like Mary, it was her expectation that generated the performance of those words said to her.

WHY THE REVELATION OF JESUS?

He Is The Way And The Reality Of The Kingdom

I am the way, the truth and the life...
John 14:6.

He Is The True Rest only available in the kingdom

Come unto me, all ye that labour and are heavy laden and I will give you rest.
Matthew 11:28.

They that have entered into rest have ceased from their own works.
Hebrews 4:10.

The bible says, "It is He that works in us both to will and to do of His good pleasure" (Philippians 2:13). What does he work in us? He works in us the realities of the kingdom.

God is working out the realities of the kingdom in you by his Spirit because it is his pleasure "...for it is the father's good pleasure to give the kingdom." Everything a child of God will ever need is contained in the kingdom, and therein lies the true rest of a Christian, but unfortunately, we have been taught everything except the kingdom, thereby majoring on the minor and focusing less on the major things that were made for our rest. Everything you will ever need to live a good life is in the kingdom.

In Matthew 18, Jesus said his kingdom was not of this world; else his army would have fought for him. In the government of the kingdom there is a defence ministry and with such you cannot be defenseless.

If He wanted to be defended from attacks and from oppression, Jesus says in His kingdom, there were Angels that would fight for Him. Angels don't just respond to you, except by the authority of the kingdom.

Doing Great Works

For we are his workmanship, created in Christ Jesus unto good works, which God hath before ordained that we should walk in them.
Ephesians 2:10.

How God anointed Jesus of Nazareth with the holy Ghost and with power who went about doing good...
Act 10:38.

We are recreated for good works and this can only be done when we are anointed as God anointed Jesus with the Holy Ghost and with power, who went about doing good and healing all that were oppressed of the devil (Acts 10:38). As the father sent Jesus so has he sent us, because He came to raise sons unto glory (John 20: 21, Hebrews 2:10), that's why it says you are His workmanship created unto good works. The good work entails miracles, signs and wonders. The bible enjoins you to, "Let your light so shine that men may see your good works..." Light is known by the manifestation of good works. You are the light of the world (Matthew 5:14), and that light is evident by good works. The function of light is not to make you pompous, but that you may be the portal through which God's dimension of mercy and glory can be seen and felt.

Raising Sons Unto Glory

The bible says He came to raise sons unto glory. Jesus is a perfect revelation of who we are. It is in our beholding Jesus that we can have the revelation of "sons raised unto glory".

Without controversy, great is the mystery of godliness, God was made manifest in the flesh
1 Timothy 3:16.

Sons of glory are manifestation of God on earth and we are called to walk in the fullness of that reality. How can you become what you don't know or see? Jesus is the perfect reference point. That is why whatever we will become must first of all be seen in the person of Jesus.

Beloved, now are we the sons of God, and it doth not yet appear what we shall be: but we know that, when he shall appear, we shall be like him; for we shall see him as he is.
1 John 3:2.

"... When he shall appear, we shall be like him..." the royalty of our sonship will come into fullness when we see Jesus as he is. Scripture further explains Sonship as 'the express image of his person, and the brightness of his glory.' (Hebrews 1:3). Sons of glory are the express image of God and the brightness of his Glory. Hence, the bible admonishes 'looking unto Jesus' who is the author and the finisher of our faith (Hebrews 12:2). It is in seeking and beholding that reality that we become like him.

In our beholding is our becoming. Our reality is limited because we lack revelation of the person of Jesus.

Appearing With Him In Glory

A story was told of an eagle's egg kept along with eggs of hen to be incubated and hatched by a mother hen. Those laid of the hen were hatched far before that of the eagle. When it was eventually hatched, the eaglet was still kept with the chicks; but she was growing at a faster rate than the chicks. The eaglet knew something was not right, realizing that its feathers were larger, however, because it had no other like it, it moved along in spite of its variation, not knowing that the chicks were raised to end up as food for its owners. Even though the eagle belongs to a class of birds referred to as king of the birds, it lived as mere chick because it didn't know its true identity.

Now I say, that the heir, as long as he is a child, differeth nothing from a servant, though he be lord of all; but is under tutors and governors until the time appointed of the father.
Galatians 4:1-2.

One day that eaglet saw another creature like itself, it realized that this creature was barely on the ground but in the air so it started to run, stretching its feathers, and before long, it was in the air, and that was how it flew back to its company and the environment it was originally created to be. The bible says "ye are gods but because ye know not, ye die as mere men" (Psalms 82:5) .When we have the revelation of Jesus, we'll begin to walk and work in our true reality. The bible says "blessed are those who love his appearing, and as many as love his appearing, to them will He appear". To those that love to see his reality, the bible says "to them will he appear", and "When he shall appear then shall ye appear with him in glory". The revelation of Jesus is not to portray the Jesus of Galilee but Jesus that appeared in his glorified state to John in Revelations. That revelation will birth in us our true reality.
That revelation was what Peter held onto. When you grasp this understanding, you'll begin to manifest a greater dimension of grace.

Wherefore gird up the loins of your mind, be sober, and hope to the end for the grace that is to be brought unto you at the revelation of Jesus Christ.
1 Peter 1:13.

There's a dimension we should walk in when we get the revelation of Jesus, and for that to happen we must be able to see Jesus from the perspective of the kingdom, not from our earthly nature.

You can't be bigger in your spiritual work than the revelation of Jesus you have. You can't be bigger in faith than your perspective of Jesus. You can't work miracles beyond the reality of Jesus you see. Therein is the reason many of us are not enjoying His fullness as we should. We can only do this by the spirit of revelation. Jesus said the Holy Spirit will take what is his and make it known unto you. The Holy Ghost is the One who reveals Him. Paul prayed a prayer that God may give you the spirit of revelation in the knowledge of Him (Ephesians 1:17). That is one of the greatest prayer a believer can pray. You can't exhaust the need for such prayer, the same way you can't exhaust the knowledge of His personality. The need and desire for the revelation of Jesus cannot be overemphasized. No! Everyday there is something new in God to know.

Even when you may think you've reached new heights, you'll still need this prayer because there are still more to be explored in him. Some of us have basked in some of His gifts. Gifts are expressions of the dimension of His reality, however there are still dimensions that ought to be explored and only our consistent walk with the Holy Spirit will give us a lifestyle that will deliver to us deeper experience of his person. The apostles went beyond gifts into a lifestyle of God's reality. Peter didn't initiate the healing by his shadow, but the people who saw his consistency with the realities of the life of Jesus and believed that his shadow was a reflection of that same reality and can manifest the same power his hands manifested, so they took advantage of it and got their sick healed. Paul also never told the people to draw healing virtue from him by the use of aprons and handkerchief. It was due to the overflow of that life. Cry for the revelation and enjoy supernatural grace.

Revealing The Three Dimensions Of Jesus

God wants to constitute Himself into us via the three dimensional positions of the person of Jesus.

Jesus The Christ And Son of God

And Simon Peter answered and said, thou art the Christ, the Son of the living God. Matthew 16:16.

Scriptures introduces him first and foremost as the Christ. You must know him first, as the Christ, the Messiah, the anointed One, the one who saves. He came to save us from our old state before we are made sons of God. Remember the Samaritan woman? She said when the Messiah comes... She wasn't expecting the Son of God but a Messiah. Several scriptures indicate that they were just expecting a Messiah. It is only by the spirit of revelation that the dimension of Christ as the son can be revealed. That is why Jesus told Peter, flesh and blood has not revealed this dimension to you but my father in heaven. So, the revelation of Jesus is progressive. He is first of all revealed as Christ. When Jesus read of himself from the writings of Isaiah, "this day is this scripture fulfilled in your ears" (Luke 4:18), demons were the first to react.

Being spirit beings they recognized Jesus as Christ and the Son of God. The demons spoke up "you are Christ the Son of God". They knew from the spiritual stand point that He was not just the Christ but also the son of God. It took a revelation from the spirit dimension for Peter to come to the same level of knowledge that the demons had. He is beyond being the Christ, he is also the Son of God. All the while the Jews were only expecting a redeemer, so they saw him as Christ, therefore never knew him as the Son of God. It must take the revelation of the Holy Spirit to see Him beyond just being the Christ.

Jesus The Son And King

After knowing him as the son of God, we must proceed to know him as king. The same Holy Spirit must reveal Him to you as King for a full revelation of who he is, else you cannot enjoy certain benefits that belong to you as a child of God. When Caiaphas asked Jesus if he was the King, it caught the attention of Jesus; for many had called him Christ and very few knew him as the son of God but Caiaphas was about the only one who thought of him as king or called him King. Jesus asked Caiaphas to know if he was merely quoting someone or he knew him as king by a personal revelation or was it based on accusation. It amazed Jesus that it had gotten to a point in his life that He was about to go, yet the people had not gotten a full revelation about Him.

A few knew Him as the Son, but the ultimate goal was for Him to be known as king, beyond being the Christ. Revelation is progressive. He was a projection of God, as the Son, but beyond that, He is God Himself, who sits on the throne as king. There is a dimension of God you enjoy when you know Him as Christ, there is another dimension you enjoy when you know Him as Son, there's yet another you enjoy when you know Him as King. Knowing Him as Christ will cause supernatural things to happen around you, but as Son, you will know Him beyond what He can do as the Christ, you will know Him as the One that can do all things through you. Knowing Him as the son is to understand your sonship. Knowing Him as King makes you reign as a king on earth as it is written, he has made us both kings and priests (Revelation 5:10). You can't understand your kingly role unless you know Him as King. All the teachings about Jesus are not meant to just reveal him as Christ or as son, but the climax is to bring us to his revelation as king.

He Is The Christ, Son and King

Now let's take a journey on the revelation of His personality as the Christ, Son and King. This is the three dimensional revelation of his person. He was born King, the wise men came asking, where is he that was born king? He was born the son of God. Isaiah 9 says "unto us a child is born, unto us a Son is given", and to Mary the bible says the child which she shall conceive shall be called the 'Son of God'. That means his office as son was declared from birth. He was also declared from birth that He would SAVE his people from sin. That stands for the Christ (savior). He was declared Christ from the beginning. At birth, He occupied those three dimensional positions but grew into full operations of the realities of these offices as he should. John the Baptist also bore witness to the fact that Jesus was the Christ at his baptism. Though he was born Christ, son and king, he had to grow into the fullness of his assignment before he was declared Christ, Son and King. Now let's see how he was declared.

And I knew him not: but that he sent me to baptize with water, the same said unto me, Upon whom thou shalt see the Spirit descending, and remaining on him, the same is he which baptizeth with the Holy Ghost.

John 1:33.

"Upon whom the Holy Ghost shall rest", signifies an ordination and pronouncement, that he is the Christ. The same place and time he was identified Christ was the same place and time he was declared son of God: "this is my son in whom I am well pleased". Then Caiaphas also acknowledged him king at crucifixion, in response to the accusation the Jews brought against him, that he calls himself king of the Jews. So he placed upon the cross the sign, 'KING OF THE JEWS'. Apart from birth, that was the second time he was declared king.

The three dimensional position of Jesus reveals the fullness of his realities. It is on the platform of the revelation of Jesus that we can teach the reality of his kingdom. Some have taught kingdom without these connections, which is why people got mere information and excitement but without result. As long as teachings on the kingdom are not sourced from the revelation of Jesus as Christ, son and king, we cant explore fully the realities of Christ available to us.

And of his fullness have all we received, and grace for grace.

John 1:16.

As earlier said, any time he appears as son, he constitutes the son in you. When he appears as Christ, he constitutes Christ in you. When he appears as king, he also constitutes the king in you. Whatever he constitutes in you is what he lives out through you. So no matter how much you pray, as long as he has not built that reality in you, you can't manifest it. Prayer aids full manifestation of his reality that you know by revelation.

The church is his body and should be the expression of God. It means no one ought to look for God in the sky, when they see us, they have seen God. The bible says, the church is the fullness of God because we have received of His fullness. (Colossians 2:9, John1:16, Ephesians 3:19). If I have received of his fullness, then I have the fullness of him as the Christ, the son and the king. God wants to walk on the earth again and he will do it through men. He will walk on earth from the three dimensional positions of his reality as Christ, Son and King.

CHAPTER 6
KINGDOM JUDICIARY SYSTEM

Just as earth has a judiciary, so also has heaven, when it sits the heaven is at attention. Its judgment is final and no one can undo it. There are factors that determine when heaven's judiciary sits. The Bible says "the kingdom of God is not in words" It's not the ability to articulate speech, but the ability to legislate and enforce laws: As Paul said to the backsliding Corinthian church in 1Corinthians 4:19 "I will come…and will know, not the speech of them which are puffed up, but the power". The church has been given an apostolic mandate, which is a governmental mandate and its function is judicial in nature.

Its major function is to legislate in line with heaven's constitution in favor of the original owner of the land.

The earth is the Lords and the fullness thereof; the world and they that dwell therein.
Psalm 24: 1.

With this in view it reveals that the assignment of the church is territorial that's why our call is ambassadorial. As an ambassador represents the interest of his country in another, so also as heaven's ambassadors, we are representatives of God's will on earth.

… be fruitful and multiply and, replenish,..subdue it and have dominion..
Genesis 1:28.

Ask of me, and I shall give thee the heathen for thine inheritance, and the uttermost parts of the earth as a possession.
Psalm 2:8.

… The kingdoms of this world are become the kingdoms of our Lord, and his Christ; and he shall reign forever and ever.
Revelation 11:15.

Subduing kingdoms until it becomes the kingdoms of our God is the sole responsibility of the church. This will be done by the church. Jesus is at the right hand of the father waiting for the church which is the battle axe of God to it is also to make His enemies his foot stool by the agency of the seven Spirits of God, which is the rod of power given to the church.

The Lord said unto my Lord, sit thou at my right hand, until I make your enemies you footstool. The lord shall send the rod of thy strength out of Zion rule thou in the mist of thine enemies.
Psalms 110:1-2.

The church is the extension of God's kingdom on earth with which it will break in pieces nations and bring them to the obedience of Christ. The evil you see on earth is the manifestation of the kingdom of darkness. One of the primary assignments of Jesus which is also the assignment of the church was to destroy the works of the enemy.

For this purpose the son of God made manifest, that he might destroy the works of the devil.
1John 3:8.

The church by extension has the same assignment; that is why Jesus said to the church to occupy till he comes. Sometimes, to occupy may necessitate a fight as David said "I am for peace but when I speak it's for war".

The church is called an occupying army, whose mission is to keep grounds already won by Christ but sometimes keeping it may require dealing with 'pockets' of demonic resistance. These resistances are the type of guerilla fighters who come in disguise as friends but their mission is to circumvent the victory Christ died for. Scripture calls them human agent or wolves in sheep clothing, ready to devour an unvigilant Christian.

Thou art my battle axe and weapons of war: for with thee will I break in pieces the nations,
and with thee will I destroy Kingdoms.
Jeremiah 51:20.

God calls you his battle axe and axe is used for executing judgment.

And In the days of these kingdoms, shall the God of heaven set up a kingdom, which shall
never be destroyed...
Daniel 2:44.

This kingdom shall take over all other kingdoms and bring them to the obedience of Christ. And this shall be made possible through understanding God's judiciary system. The Bible says "The kingdom of God is within you" that means, you are a mobile carrier of the kingdom, anywhere you go, hell submits to the lordship of Jesus through you.

Thrones

The church is not called to be famous but to serve the interest of the king. Scripture reveals the church as a kingdom of kings and priests destined to reign on earth (Revelation 5). Have you wondered why he is called the king of kings? We have been made kings and he is king over us. Every king is supposed to have a throne from where he rules from. So as kings, have you asked yourself on which throne and over what you are going to reign? The throne of God has many other thrones surrounding it. These thrones are functionaries; they are tributaries of God's eternal throne. They manifest the multifaceted dimension of God's throneroom realities. The glory of God's throne is so overwhelming and no being whether in heaven or on earth can comprehend it, hence the role of the thrones around the eternal throne of God.

And he called his ten servants, and delivered them ten pounds, and said unto them, Occupy till
I come.
Luke 19:13.

Until Jesus sees a reflection of Himself in the church, He will not come. The second coming of Jesus Christ is going to be ushered in by a people called the remnants. A people who are drunk with God's grace, a people the bible calls saviours (Obadiah 1:21), mighty men. These ones will usher His coming. He said occupy till I come. Who occupies but kings.

Christ will not come until his army goes on and secures the borders of earth. Jesus is asked to sit until his enemies are made his footstool (Psalms 110:1). Who are His footstools? Remember the bible says heaven is mine and the earth is my footstool (Isa. 66:1). That means heaven is where His kingdom dimension comes from and the earth is where it is expressed, and we are the bridge, we carry the feet. Until we take charge, he will keep on sitting.
Have you discovered that people are just hungry for more of God? It is not about them but God working out His purpose in them. God is preparing a conquering army. Like the seven thousand prophets who did not bow to Baal, (1 kings 19:18) . There are many in different lands that are hungry and burning for God. God is about to unveil an army and it is time to wake up, God is saying come up, for there are greater days ahead. Come into His sphere and into His dimension of his glory, Come into his realm come and manifest divinity in humanity. It is time for the Church to arise and take over the land, but we can't do that misaligned. Mighty men don't give themselves rest until they conquer.

What is the essence of light when it is not manifested? True light has a ripple effect. Rebecca asked, why she was having troubles within her womb, and the bible says it was because she had two nations within her. You may be carrying nations that is making you uncomfortable. It causes a restlessness, a groaning in the spirit by the Spirit (Romans 8:26).

Three Dimensional Positions Of God's Throne

God's throne appears in three forms but for the purpose of this book, we will concentrate on one which is the throne of judgment. These three thrones are:

      I. The throne of glory.
      ii. The throne of judgment.
      iii. The throne of grace.

And Jesus said unto them, verily I say unto you, that ye which have followed me, in the re-
generation when the Son of man shall sit in the throne of his glory, ye also shall sit upon
twelve thrones, judging the twelve tribes of Israel.
Matthew 19:28.

When you have a vision of the throne, you have to decipher what dimension of the throne you have come before. Paul said he went up by revelation. Revelation is the unveiling of a mystery. A mystery is something hidden for you and not from you.

For instance, a father keeps a million dollars for his two years old son but can't give him the money at that age of his life because of his myopic understanding of money. The money is kept for him until he matures. So, the father keeps it for him not from him. Maturity is not in your years but in your revelation of God's operations and alignment with his purposes. That was why Paul's greatest prayer was not for the blessing of God, because God had already blessed the church. What delivers the blessing is the revelation of everything made available by God.Throne Of Justice and Judgment. The throne of justice on which God sits reveals him as the judge of all. The nature of the throne is of justice and judgment. The kingdom of God is not complete without the judiciary arm, so also, no kingdom is complete without a place of justice and judgment, because there will be those who will disobey and oppose the order of the king. Scripture explains "he has placed those in government to judge wickedness"

Justice and judgment are the habitation of thy throne, mercy and truth shall go before they face.
Psalm 89:14.

Because of God's love for us, the throne of justice is set to protect us and the throne of judgment to establish us forever.

Of the increase of his government & peace shall be no end, upon the throne of David and upon his kingdom, to order it and establish with judgment and justice from henceforth and forever. The zeal of the Lord of hosts will perform this.
Isaiah 9:7.

God gave his throne to David, once there is a throne, there will be the realities of a kingdom. The kingdom of God in your life is established with judgment and justice; you are part of the judiciary system. You can't be established in life except by the instrumentality of justice and judgment. The throne of judgment makes you established on earth.

Kingdom authority is the mandate of all believers. But it's not expressed except establish by the revelation of judgment and justice (Job 8:3-5). God's judgment is based on the finished work of Jesus Christ: what he died and prayed for.

Blessed be the Lord thy God, which delighted in thee to set thee on his throne, to be king for the Lord thy God because thy God loved Israel.
2 Chronicles 9:8.

What Is Judgment?

Judgment is a verdict (favorable or unfavorable).

Judgment is a sentence or decision.

It is a proper fitting and execution of rules
It is the ability to discern between good and evil from God's perspective.

What is Justice?

It is uprightness.

It is the execution of judgment.

In heaven there is a supreme court, that's why He is called the judge of all, it is also the reason the Bible says we have come to the spirit of just men made perfect. "You have come to the assembly and judge of all" (Hebrews 12:22-23). An assembly gathers when the court is in session. In the book Ezekiel and Revelation, it says "the throne was set" That is, the throne is mobile. So, God's judiciary system moves around. It can move to the past, to take care of your past as though it never existed and make you enter into the future with blessing as though it was originally programmed to be so.

The children of Israel who came out with silver and gold got justice for their labor. They were paid for their years of slavery in one day. If what you have lost is not restored when justice is served, then something is wrong because it ensures restoration. This is how God's judiciary system works. "If a thief is caught he's meant to pay seven folds".

You are part of that judiciary system and there must be fair judgment. Paul said "don't you know you would judge angels?" That is how powerful a believer is. As a believer you are part of the host of heaven which is part of the judiciary council of heaven (2 Chronicles 18:18).

> *... And every tongue that shall rise against thee in judgment thou shall condemn. This is the heritage of the servants of the Lord, and their righteousness is of me, saith the Lord.*
> *Isaiah 54:17;*

Satan is supposed to be working for you, to punish your enemies not you.

He is supposed to be your servant (I Corinthians 5:3) but he works against believers with filthy garments. Satan had the right to stand close to Joshua because he had a filthy garment (Zachariah 3:1). Demons also have the right to justice when you have their property; when you have sin in you. Until the filthy garment was removed the angel of the lord could not stand by to defend him.

CHAPTER 7
KINGDOM DEFENCE SYSTEM

God has an eternal purpose that should be our priority for as long as we live, so that our lives can progressively conform to it: our entire lives should be the expression of God's eternal purpose here on earth. The reason we make decrees and wage war in the spirit is to enforce the purposes of God and not for selfish end, else, we will pray amiss.

> *Ye ask, and receive not, because ye ask amiss, that ye may consume it upon your lusts.*
> *James 4:3.*

His Eternal Purpose

You are not here for yourself but for a divine assignment and it must be registered in your heart. Your essence of existence is his eternal purpose. As God's servant, you should not die before your appointed time especially when you have his eternal purpose at heart. Paul said he had a choice of going to rest with God but felt it was better he remained on earth. God's agenda on earth was stronger than his comfort.

We are getting to the close of the age where things are being wrapped up. It's like the church above is about to become one with the church on earth. The earthly pattern is about to be overtaken by the Heavenly pattern.

When the bible mentions the end of the world, it doesn't mean the end of creation, it means the end of an age, so that His own age will come in. The book of Revelation says a new heaven and a new earth came down, which means an age will end. The bible says this world will not end until the gospel is preached. The 'end of the world' is not the end of the whole creation but the end of an age, the end of cosmos.

Cosmos shall be conquered, subdued, and brought under. That is why God is stirring up His army. What is happening to the world right now is a reflection of what is happening in the spirit because there's about to be a close of the evil age, and that is not going to be by rapture but by the church subduing evil. It will close cosmos and will subdue it.

God's Occupying Army

> *And he called his ten servants, and delivered them ten pounds, and said unto them, Occupy till I come.*
> *Luke 19:13.*

The church must occupy till He comes. And to make that possible on the earth, we must overcome our selfish desires because we can't conquer the world when we have not conquered self. God is stirring up our hearts towards taking over territories Satan had held siege. A take-over mentality must rest upon the church now and not just a mentality of prosperity that is void of kingdom agenda.

Cry yet, saying, Thus saith the Lord of hosts; My cities through prosperity shall yet be spread abroad; and the Lord shall yet comfort Zion, and shall yet choose Jerusalem.
Zechariah 1:17.

It is all about the advancement of God's kingdom, and as the bible says "of the increase of that kingdom there shall be no end…" This kingdom is the invincible government of God upon the earth. It is the influence of God's government upon the earth poised to taking over the hearts of men and territories.

The earth is the LORD's, and the fullness thereof, the world, and they that dwelleth in it.
Psalms 24:1.

Activating Kingdom Defense

Until all the manipulation and strength of evil is conquered, cosmos is not conquered. As every country has a defense department or ministry which is supposed to defend its territory. So also, the church is God's army and they are responsible for the defense and enlargement of God's kingdom on earth. They are at the expense of the commanding officer.

What is an Army?

It is a collection of soldiers. A soldier is one who has signed his death warrant before his enlistment, to protect the territory of his country. He comes in not to do his own will but that of the one who enlisted him.

Be Conscious Of His Eternal Purpose

Thou therefore endure hardness, as a good soldier of Jesus Christ.
2 Timothy 2:3.

That means we also have bad soldiers, people that forget the eternal purpose, those who seem to lose consciousness of his assignment. A bad soldier is like Achan who was supposed to go and destroy a city, but went in and forgot his assignment, his selfish motive overtook him and he ended up bringing harm to the children of Israel. A good soldier does not forget his assignment. He lives only to fulfill his mandate.

No man that warreth entangleth himself with the affairs of thislife; that he may please him who hath chosen him to be a soldier.
2 Timothy 2:4.

The pursuit of a good soldier is to please his commander. The reason we destroy evil is not for our sake but that God's eternal purpose be fulfilled. David said,

I shall not die but live and declare the works of the Lord.
Psalms 118:17.

Our safety is guaranteed when we abide to the desire and instructions of the commander. As we target God's target, we will not be victims of Satan's target.

...touch not my anointed and do my prophet no harm
Psalms 105:15.

I am the anointed of the Lord. He has anointed me to preach the gospel. As long as I keep to my divine assignment, my preservation is guaranteed. Angels become my backup and partner to seeing to the expansion of the kingdom. Every choice I make, must be in favor of enriching the purposes of God on the earth.

Effectiveness In Prayer

If the reason we serve God is for selfish end, our prayer will not be effective. One of the keys to effective prayer is that you present kingdom oriented reasons but when some people pray and don't get results it was due wrong reason in prayer. They seem to forget that scripture says "...bring forth your strong reason." If your reason does not comply with God's eternal purpose, it is not a reason.

If the reason you want to live long has no eternal purpose, it is useless. Long life is the privilege of every believer but it has to be tied to eternal purpose, so that the gospel can be spread. So at seventy, God can say concerning you, 'this guy is doing well, let's give him fifty more years.' Hezekiah gave God a strong reason to live and God added fifteen more years to his age. Hezekiah did not base his reason on the fact that some king lived a hundred years.

God is correcting that wrong motive, else you will have a problem later. You can quickly repent as you read on. That is why the strength of the kingdom will not be seen until your heart is right.

... And all these things shall be added unto you.
Matthew 6:33.

Once it is not about the kingdom, there is a problem. A true soldier lives and dies for one course; his whole life, well being, everything is for that course. When some soldiers in my country were court-marshaled, I was one of the people complaining, in fact, I was upholding one of them in prayers. But I latter found out that they were court marshaled because they left the battle ground on the bases of not being provided with enough weapons. I guess they forgot that they signed to defend their country with their lives. So with good or bad weapons, they ought to have fought and protected the territory of their country. That was what they signed for.

Be Committed To His Eternal Purpose

In the military set up when commanded, your choice is not considered. That was the kind of army Alexander the Great had. Once the commanding officer gives a command, you must not do otherwise. The bible says he that shall love his life shall lose it, and he that shall lose his life shall save it. Nowadays, Christianity is that of convenience and that is why we don't have the results the saints of old had. When rebuked, you get angry and leave the church. How can such a person become a strong Christian? How can you be trusted with eternal powers? And you are supposed to be dealing with the powers of the age to come. The bible says if you are unfaithful with mammon, how can you be entrusted with eternal things? So when people begin to give excuses, it is an expression of the state of their hearts.

The journey of a believer is a sacrifice, laying down his life and going all the way for the King. Until such a church is raised, Jesus Christ is not coming back. He is coming for a church without spot, that spot is not just sin. It means that their flesh does not play a role in hindering God's purpose. They are not ruled by the flesh but by the spirit. This is the meaning of 'without spot or wrinkles.' I sometimes deliberately test people, to know whether their heart is right. The church of the last day is not one that complacency should come in. that is why I said you must have conviction and you must know what you are living for. Many will misinterpret my action but it doesn't matter, pleasing the chief commanding officer is my goal.

Jesus answered, My kingdom is not of this world: if my kingdom were of this world, then would my servants fight, that I should not be delivered to the Jews: but now is my kingdom not from hence.
John 18:36.

He said if my kingdom were of this world, then would my servant's fight, that means his kingdom has fighters too. Revelation 12 says there was war in heaven, Michael and his angels fought against the dragon, and they fought to a point that the bible says there was no place again for him. So combat is normal in the spiritual realm. There is an army in heaven answerable to God's eternal purpose. The hosts of God in heaven are the angels, the cherubs, the seraphim, and saints alike. The bible says "He maketh His ministers flame of fire" (Hebrews 1:7). They were made from fire. "He maketh them" and their work is to execute the written judgment. If you think Jesus came to play, you are mistaken because, He was brutal and forceful against demonic orchestrations. He was not totally gentle as portrayed when it came to kingdom business.

When we talk about a defense system, it entails executing judgment and punishment upon the heathen. Sometimes chaos cannot be stabilized except by executing judgment. In fact chaos itself is a type of war against peace. The bible says the earth was without form and void, so there was a form of war before the spirit of God moved upon it. Life does not come to stability except there is a form of war in the spirit. The Psalmist said.

I am for peace: but when I speak, they are for war.
Psalms 120:7.

God's Roar Is the Judgment of the Enemy

Look at Jesus, He didn't come peacefully. I was shocked when I saw it.

And Jesus said, for judgment I am come into this world, that they which see not might see; and that they which see might be made blind.
John 9:39.

He came to cosmos to judge it. In first John 3:8 it says "...For this purpose the Son of God was manifested, that he might destroy..." He came for judgment, but how did He do it? He had to destroy! There had to be war in the heavenly. You can't have judgment without punishment. I read something by a man of God who said dialogue cannot solve all the problems of the world and that is true. When we dialogue, we may still come back to fight, because one may attempt to undermine the agreement. Not all land disputes has ever been resolved between nations by dialogue, sometimes it takes judgment to resolve such disputes. The nature of kingdom is enlargement and taking over territories. He said I came for judgment, and for that to be executed, you must war against spiritual forces in the heavenly. And the One who backs this judgment is the commander in chief of the host of heaven, the Lion of the tribe of Judah, and the bible says He has prevailed.

Will a lion roar in the forest, when he hath no prey?

> *Will a young lion cry out of his den, if he have taken nothing?*
> *Amos 3:4.*

So there is a cry and it's a cry of battle, it's a cry of war. The bible says every battle is with confused noise and that noise is a noise of war. It causes confusion in the camp of the enemy. There is a shaking, there is something happening. There's an army God is raising.

The lion hath roared, who will not fear?
The Lord GOD hath spoken, who can but prophesy?

Why are we prophesying these things? Because God has roared, that was why when John was crying in Revelation, he was told the Lion of the tribe of Judah has prevailed (Revelation 5:5). The roar is a sign of victory. It's a language of victory. That roar is the victory that was prophesied.

> *And cried with a loud voice, as when a lion roareth:*
> *And when he had cried, seven thunders uttered their voices.*
> *Revelation 10:3.*

When the lion roars, thunders utter their voices. That means the lion's roar brings forth seven dimensions of thunders, which means perfect judgment.

> *For every battle of the warrior is with confused noise, and garments rolled in blood; but this*
> *shall be with burning and fuel of fire.*
> *Isaiah 9:5.*

Our commanding Officer is that Lion and when he roars, the kingdom of darkness rattles. When the Lion roars, things happen. upon his roar, the angels win battles. The bible says they prevailed, they overcame him and Satan had no more place in heaven.

When we do warfare prayer in tongues, It is a roar of confused noise. Isaiah 9:5 says the noise of the battle is a confused noise. When you pray in tongues, do it with an understanding; it is the release of voices of thunders through tongues. Your tongue is a language of the spirit. It's actually a roar. Anytime tongues go into warfare, it is actually the Lion roaring, the Commanding Officer roaring through you and doing terrible things.

And the great dragon was cast out, that old serpent, called the Devil, and Satan, which deceiveth the whole world: he was cast out into the earth, and his angels were caste out with him. And I heard a loud voice saying in heaven, now is come salvation, and strength, and the kingdom of our God, and the power of his Christ: for the accuser of our brethren is cast down, which accused them before our God day and night.
Revelation 12:9-10.

Amos 3:4 says how can a lion roar when there is no pray, how can a young lion roar if he has not caught anything? Everything attacking you will become a prey in your hands and there will be judgment upon the wicked. Jesus said for judgment have I come. "that He might destroy the works of the enemy" He can't fulfill His ministry without destroying the works of the enemy. Like I said, there can't be justice without judgment, because justice is the execution of judgment. There is a roar in the realm of the spirit already and it will begin to have effect on our immediate environment.

Scripture says there is no sound without a meaning. You will notice a stirring in your spirit. Why? It is a stir to pray and wait upon the Lord. It is because there is a roar in the spirit and our ability to synchronize with the sound of heaven will make us have major victories on the face of the earth.

Do As Jesus Did

Jesus said as I see my Father do, so do I. When father is judging, Jesus is judging. He said I came for judgment, so God was judging. When we willingly open up our spirit, we become sensitive to the activities going on in heaven. Many fail in life because of the inability to know when they are called to war in prayers. When a believer is sensitive, the happenings in the Spirit concerning him will bear witness upon his spirit, so that he knows what to do at every season. In judges, Gideon was to align himself to win his battles, he was told "when you see the wind blow upon the mulberry tree, do as occasion demands of you." When you see the Spirit of God begin to move in a direction, do as occasion demands of you.

The Spirit of the Lord came upon Samson and he suddenly became brutal. Any time the spirit came upon him, he knew that God wanted him to destroy Satan's stronghold. It is time the Church rise up to its kingdom responsibility. The church is God's army on the face of the earth. Bear in mind that there are angelic beings that go to war any time we obey the clarion call to war in prayers. One of these angels in record is what we saw in revelation with one leg on earth, one in the sea and his face as of the sun. Upon his head is like rainbow. Can you see how mighty this being is? You have been empowered to reign over the activities of wickedness.

You must understand that the kinds of angels that attend Church meetings are determined by the nature of the meeting. When a meeting for warfare is to hold, the angels in charge of war are majorly present. Angels of finance are rarely found in such meetings. Heaven wants to fight for God's eternal purpose.

> *The king's wrath is as the roaring of a lion; but his favor is as dew upon the grass.*
> *Proverbs 19:12.*

So when God is angry, He roars and when He does so, it is the release of voices of seven thunders. In Psalm 2, the bible says "kiss" the prince less he be angry with you and ye perish. God told us He is angry and jealous over His people. When God is jealous over you, things will change in your favor.

> *They shall walk after the LORD: he shall roar like a lion: when he shall roar, then the*
> *children shall tremble from the west.*
> *Hosea 11:10.*

God's Defense Executes Judgment through You

God is about to roar, he said I should tell His people not to weep because the Lion has prevailed. He is going to roar again, and the activities of the enemy in your life is about to receive total judgment.

> *And I say also unto thee, That thou art Peter, and upon this rock I will build my church; and*
> *the gates of hell shall not prevail against it.*
> *Matthew 16:18.*

How?

> *And I will give unto thee the keys of the kingdom of heaven: and whatsoever thou shalt bind*
> *on earth shall be bound in heaven: and whatsoever thou shalt loose on earth shall be loosed in*
> *heaven.*
> *Matthew 16:19.*

That is how the defense system of God operates. It empowers God's people to bind and lose, they determine things, and execute judgment. When we talk about the defense, we talk about execution-doing terrible things in righteousness, and Heaven will do that through you.

> *Thou art my battle axe and weapons of war: for with thee will I break in pieces the nations,*
> *and with thee will I destroy kingdoms.*
> *Jeremiah 51:20.*

The bible is referring to the heathens when it mentions nations. When I looked at the meaning, it was referring to foreigners. Whatever is foreign in your life is described here as heathen and nation in psalms 2, and it say with thee I will break "the nations. How will He do that?

> *Behold, I will make thee a new sharp threshing instrument having teeth…*

Isaiah 41:15.

God says we are His battle axe and weapons of war. But He has to sharpen these weapons of war to be effectively destroy nations.

You have to allow Him make you. Samson couldn't kill a fly but the bible says when the Spirit of the Lord came upon him, he tore a lion like a kid. When the Spirit of God comes upon you, you do what you couldn't do. He sharpens you. He gives you a tongue of fire so that when you speak it will be judgment. The bible says by the word of your mouth you shall be justified or condemned. Say this loud: I've been made a new sharp threshing instrument having teeth.

Scripture says having spoilt principalities and powers, He made a show of them. We are going to clean up what has been finished by the commander in chief through playing our roll as God's occupying army. One of the things we do as God's occupying army is to protect the territory which was secured by the blood of the lamb. That is why if a Christian has a blood line around him, and that blood shields him from the enemy. For that evil situation to have persisted shows that you are not angry enough to change it. Even the enemy knows that you are eternally his master, but he is taking advantage of your lack of seriousness and lack of anger against it. Whatever you are not angry about, you cannot change. Anything you leave unchecked will breathe again. God is raising an army that is brutal. That brutality is why Psalm 82: refers to them as gods who are not supposed to watch wickedness persist.

God standeth in the congregation of the mighty; he judgeth among the gods. How long will ye judge unjustly, and accept the persons of the wicked? Selah. Defend the poor and fatherless: do justice to the afflicted and needy. Deliver the poor and needy: rid them out of the hand of the wicked.

I have said, ye are gods; and all of you are children of the most high.
Psalm 82:1-4,6.

The bible says whatever we bind on earth shall be bound in heaven. It is time to arise and put the enemy where he belongs.

Blow ye the trumpet in Zion, and sound an alarm in my holy mountain: let all the inhabitants of the land tremble: for the day of the Lord cometh, for it is nigh at hand; A day of darkness and of gloominess, a day of clouds and of thick darkness, as the morning spread upon the mountains: a great people and a strong; there hath not been ever the like, neither shall be any more after it, even to the years of many generations. A fire devoureth before them; and behind them a flame burneth: the land is as the garden of Eden before them, and behind them a desolate wilderness; yea, and nothing shall escape them. The appearance of them is as the appearance of horses; and as horsemen, so shall they run. Like the noise of chariots on the tops of mountains shall they leap, like the noise of a flame of fire that devoureth the stubble, as a strong people set in battle array. Before their face the people shall be much pained: all faces shall gather blackness. They shall run like mighty men; they shall climb the wall like men of war; and they shall march everyone on his ways, and they shall not break their ranks.
Joel 2:1-7.

Waging War

Paul said I write to you son Timothy on the importance of warfare in prophecy.

This charge I commit unto thee, son Timothy, according to the prophecies which went before on thee, that thou by them mightest war a good warfare.
1 Timothy 1:18.

Fight the good fight of faith, lay hold on eternal life, whereunto thou art also called, and hast professed a good profession before many witnesses.
1 Timothy 6:12.

Kingdom defense entails waging war. No one in a war entangles himself with civilians' affairs. So we are in a war. If you check, every believer was born before battle line and should carry the character of the army in the book of Joel. They are nameless, they are faceless, they are fearless, they are not weak, they are unconquerable, and they are powerful, mighty, and strong. They do terrible things. They look like lions, they run like horsemen.

It is time to take over, take over lost territories, and take over what belongs to you. Don't sit down and allow your life go down the drain. A generation has risen that has refused to live in the shadows of its fathers. It has made up its mind to walk in the reality of what belongs to it. They will do like the mighty men of David, taking over territories.

But he answered and said, every plant, which my heavenly Father hath not planted, shall be rooted up.
Matthew 15:13.

Behold, I give unto you power to tread on serpents and Scorpions, and over all the power of the enemy: and nothing Shall by any means hurt you.
Luke 10:19.

This honor has been given to the saints to execute the written judgment. Executing judgment is part of righteousness. This is what we call righteous judgment. If you don't move evil things out, they will move you out of the world.

CHAPTER 8
KINGDOM FINANCE SYSTEM

God wants to empower us financially. Prosperity is one empowerment we need in the body of Christ.

Cry yet, saying, Thus saith the Lord of hosts; My cities through prosperity shall yet be spread abroad; and the Lord shall yet comfort Zion, and shall yet choose Jerusalem.
Zechariah 1:17.

True prosperity has its root in God. Whatever is not sourced from God has no durability and can not stand the economy melt down affecting the world. God delights in your prosperity and wants to bless you from the riches of his glory. It doesn't matter how bad your life has been. Your connection with the kingdom is your connection to God's wealth. Remember Everything in Heaven and on Earth belongs to the King and He delights in the prosperity of His people (the church). The king is so rich that He says he would supply all our needs according to His riches in Glory. There is no amount of hard work in this life that can supply all your needs but the King can.

... The earth is the Lord's and the fullness thereof...
Psalms 24:1.

For every beast of the forest is mine, and the cattle upon a thousand hills.
Psalms 50: 10.

When you amass things and you are still afraid, it is a sign that you are not enjoying the true prosperity of God's Kingdom.

Everything that comes from God bears the nature and character of God's kingdom. So, the prosperity that comes from God only increases and comes with peace, as a reflection of the King from whom the prosperity comes.

The blessing of the Lord, it maketh rich, and he addeth no sorrow with it.
Proverbs 10:22.

The righteous shall flourish like the palm tree: he shall grow like a cedar in Lebanon.
Psalm 92:12.

Despite your hard work, as long as it is not given to you from that Kingdom it will pass away. Things of the Kingdom are shrouded in mysteries. They are deep things. Everything that comes from God is as deep as God; you must go through God to fetch them. It is only the things you get from God that don't depreciate but everything you get elsewhere depreciates. Economic melt down has no effect in the Kingdom. The blessings of God are like water of sea there is no amount of water you fetch from the sea that can make it dry.

John answered and said, A man can receive nothing, except it be given him from heaven.
John 3:27.

Kingdom Wealth Transfer And Creation

The coming wealth is going to be via two means; Kingdom wealth transfer and Kingdom wealth creation.Wealth means having everything that pertains to life and Godliness. It is wealth creation that brought about the creation of coin in the mouth of the fish when Jesus was expected to pay tax.

Notwithstanding, lest we should offend them, go thou to the sea, and cast an hook, and take up the fish that first cometh up; and when thou hast opened his mouth, thou shalt find a piece of money: that take, and give unto them for me and thee.
Matthew 17:27.

It is also wealth creation that brought about the multiplication of two fishes and five loaves of bread.

And he commanded the multitude to sit down on the grass, and took the five loaves, and the two fishes, and looking up to heaven, he blessed, and brake, and gave the loaves to his disciples, and the disciples to the multitude. And they did all eat, and were filled: and they took up of the fragments that remained twelve baskets full.
Matthew 14:19-20.

Money can be created. The power that can give you wealth is in God's kingdom; as such if you can access it by revelation then you can have it.

He answered and said unto them, because it is given unto you to know the mysteries of the kingdom of heaven, but to them it is not given.
Matthew 13:11.

These mysteries are called the keys of the kingdom. If they are not given to you, you cannot have them irrespective of the person that preaches to you.

If Spiritual things must be given to you, they won't come by just listening to messages. If the revelation behind it is not opened to you, it cannot profit you. It will only remain a powerful theory, regardless of the man of God that preached to you. How well it works for you is also dependent on the perception of your heart. The Holy Ghost works with an understandable heart.

Need for the Spirit of Understanding

The eyes of your understanding being enlightened; that ye may know what is the hope of his
calling, and what the riches of the glory of his inheritance in the saints.
Ephesians 1:18.

As a result, you must learn to prepare your heart by speaking and praying in the Spirit, this aids your understanding. For the Word of God is Spirit and must first be planted in your spirit before it materializes.

... and the Word became flesh and dwelt among men.
John 1:14.

The Holy Ghost helps to prepare your heart so that when the Word falls on it, it can produce the desired result. The problem of life is never about the Word of God but the heart, because the Word is ever potent but the heart has to be ready to receive it. The strength of every Kingdom is known by the strength of its wealth and defense system. It actually begins with the economy. Jesus the King of this Kingdom carries the grace of wealth. The essence of this wealth is that the Kingdom of God can spread abroad.

Anointing For Wealth

But thou shalt remember the Lord thy God: for it is he that giveth thee power to get wealth, that he may establish his covenant which he sware unto thy fathers, as it is this day.
Deuteronomy 8:18.

There is an anointing that brings prosperity, until that grace or anointing rests upon you, you will only work very hard, yet not be wealthy. Joseph prospered and caused Potiphar's house to prosper because he had the grace of prosperity upon him. Working hard to make wealth is not the key rather it is heaven's empowerment. Understanding the role of the anointing is very important. Without light on how God's kingdom wealth operates, you may be lost in the darkness of poverty.

Light is in different degrees. Understanding is light, wisdom is light and revelation is light but in different frequencies.

Arise shine, for you light has come and the Glory of the Lord is risen upon thee.
Isaiah 60:1.

In the Kingdom of God we strive by the economy of light. Scripture says "for your light has come" and it's based on that light that the Glory of God shall be obvious upon you.
The Light of God when received has the capacity to draw wealth and favor to you, in Isaiah 60:2-3. We will see the various dimensions of abundance that light compels. It explains why Paul prayed "... the eyes of your understanding be flooded with light." Ephesians 1:18. When light comes to a believer, every good thing pulls toward him.

For, behold, the darkness shall cover the earth, and gross darkness the people: but the Lord shall arise upon thee, and his glory shall be seen upon thee. And the Gentiles shall come to thy light, and kings to the brightness of thy rising.
Isaiah 60:2-3.

Darkness is not a factor when light is available, it is your light that the Gentiles shall come to, bringing in their wealth.

And the Gentiles shall come to thy light, and kings to the brightness of thy rising. Lift up thine eyes round about, and see: all they gather themselves together, they come to thee: thy sons shall come from far, and thy daughters shall be nursed at thy side. Then thou shalt see, and flow together, and thine heart shall fear, and be enlarged; because the abundance of the sea shall be converted unto thee, the forces of the Gentiles shall come unto thee.
Isaiah 60: 3-5.

In the Glory, the forces of the Gentiles shall be converted to you. Observing the above scripture, there's no place where it is stated that you will go and look for wealth, rather it will be drawn to you. Working hard to get wealth is not God's ultimate way of making us wealthy, this further explains what Abraham understood and why he rejected payment from men when he helped them defeat their enemy, so that his riches is not the result of hard work or human connection. It is God's power; it is He that empowers a man to make wealth.

But thou shalt remember the Lord thy God: for it is he that giveth thee power to get wealth, that he may establish his covenant which he sware unto thy fathers, as it is this day.
Deuteronomy 8:18.

Man's need for prosperity is so important that it has become an easy tool to distract him from destiny. See what Satan did, scripture says he took Jesus to the top of the pinnacle to show Him the Kingdom of the world and all its Glory in a moment.

Satan knew he could make man compromise on the ground of wealth. That was why he took Him so high so He could view all the wealth of the kingdom from one spot. Jesus didn't fall to Satan's trick for he knew the true owner of all things.

The multitude of camels shall cover thee, the dromedaries of Midian and Ephah; all they from Sheba shall come: they shall bring gold and incense; and they shall shew forth the praises of the Lord. All the flocks of Kedar shall be gathered together unto thee. The rams of Nabaioth shall minister unto thee. They shall come up with acceptance on my altar, and I glorify the house of my Glory.
Isaiah 60: 6-7.

The Lord is empowering his house with wealth. Individually and collectively as a church (the house of His Glory) Get ready! I see God turning ordinary people into wealthy people.

Lack Is Not A Sign Of Holiness

… And God led them out with Silver and Gold.

Psalm 105:35.

God is not anti-prosperity. Do you know that even the Holiest of all was made of gold? Poverty is not righteousness, neither is your lack a sign of holiness. Some think to become poorer, is to become Holier: the poorer they become the holier they become.

Who are these that fly as cloud, and as the doves to their windows ... the Isles shall wait for me and the sheep of Tarshish first, to bring the sons from afar, their silver and their gold with them. Unto the name of the Lord thy God, and to the Holy one of Israel because He hath Glorified thee.
Isaiah 60:8-9.

God wants to glorify the church in wealth...

And the sons of strangers shall build up thy walls, and their kings shall minister unto thee: for in my wrath I smote thee, but in my favor have I had mercy. Therefore thy gate shall be open continually... I will make thee an eternal Excellency.

This is the wealth the Lord wants to give to his church not the type that comes by the sweat of the brow but by covenant and obedience. We saw in Isaiah 60 how forces will come in continually. I call this 'good embarrassment.' It will be coming continually until you have no room for more. That is what it means to be blessed from His riches of glory. And. If God didn't consult World Bank to bless Solomon, then don't you think He will not fail when he says He will give you the riches of the Gentiles?

How do you explain the famine in the land of Samaria? It became so bad that the people began to eat each other's children. That was the greatest recession the world ever had. Yet, God changed their situation within some hours.

Can a woman forget her suckling child..?
Isaiah 49:15.

But this time, they forgot their suckling children. Poverty is bad! When you see a woman give her children for witchcraft, it is poverty. There is no place witchcraft thrives like Africa, and it is because of poverty. The benefit of the death of Jesus on the cross is enough for the church. I do not need to shed any blood for wealth He has paid it all for me and you.

Trust not Uncertain Riches

The wealth of this world is called uncertain riches.

Charge them that are rich in this world, they be not high minded, nor trust in uncertain riches...
1Timothy6:17.

Psalms 73:3 calls it the prosperity of the wicked. Anything you gather by labor; by the system of this world, the system of cosmos, the Bible calls it the prosperity of the wicked.

... The prosperity of the wicked.
Psalm 73:3.

Why is it the prosperity of fools? Because it is by the wisdom of the world... the Bible says the world by its wisdom does not know God. It's a perverted wisdom. This wisdom by which they gather wealth is what is called the wisdom of this world and it gives what the bible refers to as the prosperity of fools and the prosperity of fools destroys them (Psalms 73:1-2).The Bible also calls such prosperity, the prosperity of the wicked. Whatever is not given to you from above will not stand the test of time.

This is the portion of a wicked man with God, and the heritage of oppressors, which they shall receive of the Almighty. If his children be multiplied, it is for the sword: and his offspring shall not be satisfied with bread. Those that remain of him shall be buried in death: and his widows shall not weep. Though he heap up silver as the dust, and prepare raiment as the clay; He may prepare it, but the just shall put it on, and the innocent shall divide the silver.
Job27:13-17.

For God giveth to a man that is good in his sight wisdom, and knowledge, and joy: but to the sinner he giveth travail, to gather and to heap up, that he may give to him that is good before God. This also is vanity and vexation of spirit.
Ecclesiastes 2:26.

God's assignment to the wicked is to gather and to heap up that he may give to them that are good before God. This is how transfers are made. When David realized this, he knew there was no wisdom envying the wicked. He said he was almost gone but when He saw the end and what will happen to the wicked, he retrieved himself. He decided to keep a clean heart and followed God's patterned principles for prosperity.
His principle is the opposite to the world's principles and you will need to change the way you think for you to acces kingdom wealth. Those who have tried to out smart kingdom wealth principles have only been smitten by poverty.

So this Daniel prospered in the reign of Darius, and in the reign of Cyrus the Persian.
Daniel 6:28.

These kings were unbelievers yet Daniel prospered under their ledership . No matter what religion the President of the country is practicing, it does not count in the Kingdom. It does not matter who is the owner or the boss of the organization where you work, when God wants to bless you, he does that regardless. Daniel prospered and reigned in the days of these gentile kings. Others struggled but Daniel prospered. It doesn't matter the economic meltdown, you will prosper. Daniel understood he had a covenant. The covenant is independent on who is around you. The force backing the kingdom draws wealth to you.

Think, Confess Wealth

Think and talk like a kingdom person. Your confession is ruled by what you think. If you say the economy is bad, you empower the economy to be bad and you attract such because you are a product of your thought and utterance.

> *... as a man thinketh in his heart...*
> *Proverbs 23:7.*

CHAPTER 9
HOW TO ACCESS KINGDOM WEALTH

Kingdom wealth is heart related. God's wealth only tends to those who have eternal purpose in their hearts. They have the program and agenda of Heaven at the back of their minds. As scripture says, give and it shall be given to you. It's not just the giving but what prompts you to give. That is the first condition for wealth - the state of your heart.

The State Of Your Heart

In God's Kingdom, you don't go after wealth, it comes after you. You seek the Kingdom primarily and every other thing will be added to you. Not just Kingdom, but its righteousness. That means, the right way things should be done. Don't just go for the Kingdom but also do its bids. People don't prosper in the Kingdom because they don't seek the kingdom and its righteousness.

> *Ye ask, and receive not, because ye ask amiss...*
> *James 4:3.*

Only things that have eternal value draw the blessing of Heaven. The eternal plan of God must be first. Not just for the sake of what you can get.

> *And ye shall serve the Lord your God, and he shall bless thy bread, and thy water; and I will take sickness away from the midst of thee. There shall nothing cast their young, nor be barren, in thy land: the number of thy days I will fulfill.*
> *Exodus 23:25.*

A young rich man came to Jesus wanting to know how he could be part of God's kingdom. Jesus told him to go and give his riches to the poor; but when he heard that, he became discouraged and left. That was a test of his love for the kingdom. That shows you where his love was. If you love the Kingdom, obeying its demands should not be a problem.

The Bible clearly states that, he was sorrowful because he was very rich. His quest was not based on his love for the King but obviously for his own personal interest. God was not against his wealth, but God wanted to give him a heart check to prove if his heart quest was genuine. Your giving is the expression of the state of your heart. It is also the expression of your love for God. Let's take Abraham as an example

> *And he said, Take now thy son, thine only son Isaac, whom thou lovest, and get thee into the land of Moriah; and offer him there for a burnt offering upon one of the mountains which I will tell thee of.*
> *Genesis 22:2.*

Bible says, Abraham left the following morning and walked for three days before he found the mountain. He did not forget any material necessary for the sacrifice. He didn't consult Sarah, else, there would have been a struggle because the love of a mother would have been a distraction to him. All He told her was that they were going to worship God.

The ability to overcome self is an act of worship. He took the boy and laid him upon the altar of sacrifice. You may say God knows my heart, but God was also seeing Abraham's heart when he commanded him to offer Isaac as a sacrifice. When Abraham was about to thrust the knife into Isaac, God said stop it! Now I know that you love me.

The Bible says no good will he withhold from those that love him. But every love must be proven in the Kingdom. You may be singing and jumping. God will appreciate you but will still insist that you prove it. Every time you say God you know I love you, he will bring a test. The Bible says, no greater love than this, than for you to lay your life for your friend. Do you love him enough to want to die for him? If you worship the things you possess, it means that your life cannot be touched. The moment you begin to murmur and cry, God will place a question mark on your love. It does not take time, it takes obedience; the time is never a factor when God is set to prosper a man because he can prosper anybody, anytime. That is why there are young millionaires now.

All you need is to pass your love test. That is why when you say 'I love God' he insists that there must be a test of that love.

Praise ye the Lord. Blessed is the man that feareth the Lord, that delighteth greatly in his commandments.
Psalms 112:1.

Love brings you to the place of obedience. Any man who loves God has great delight in his commandment. Whatever God says, is final. God can't entrust you when He can't take things from you. You may be wondering why God is not blessing some people. I will show you why: the bible says, you don't give precious things to swine... The riches of God are eternal that is when it is given to you, your life changes forever. God will not give, until He checks the heart. Even Jesus got to a point that God laid a demand on him. He said, Lord, nevertheless, not my will but thine. Sometime the demand of God will hurt you and cost you everything. It doesn't take Him anything to empower a man, but the price is the heart.

His seed shall be mighty upon earth: the generation of the upright shall be blessed. Wealth and riches shall be in his house; and his righteousness endureth forever.
Psalm 112:2-3.

Heart Check

Your heart is the most important factor to enjoying Kingdom wealth. As a result, if there is an opportunity to give in order to be blessed, its wisdom to check your motive for giving and prove your love for God. As a believer, I always do a heart check. Your seed or sacrifice can be offensive to God with a bad condition of heart.

God is set to bless His people. Wherever you are required to give, do it as an act of obedience to God and the expression of your love for him. Some people are going to be the Solomon of their generation but they must pass the love test. Your lifting will be determined by your love for God.

Bishop David Oyedepo gave so much in love to God to the point that God said even if you want to be poor, you cannot be anymore. And the evidence is there. Can you suspend your need for the sake of the Kingdom? It is an act of love. I can sacrifice anything. I have never seen anybody who sacrificially gave his time and money and regretted it. It has never happened. In scripture, neither will it happen in your time.

When God sees the level of your obedience, love and sacrifice for His kingdom, He opens doors of favor for you. There are times God will require from you. "…Thine only child, whom thou lovest". There are sacrifices that moves God for your favor and delivers you from the attacks of your enemies. At such times, God becomes the enemy of your enemies.

Be Wise!

Never allow prosperity messages be the stimulant for your giving. . Instead of waiting to be cajoled, you can ask God to cultivate the 'giving heart' in you. It is about the heart. I prayed to God not to give me anything I can't give back to Him. Some people today follow after preachers who will give them what their ears are itching after. But Jesus gave the people raw truth and many left Him. They wanted to make Him King because of the benefit not because they believe he deserves it. If a pastor is not ready to lose his members based on the truth, he has not started ministry. I have come to the point where I am ready to obey God regardless of the number of the members I have.

Live And Give Sacrificially

Scriptures says, I have never seen the righteous forsaken nor seen his seed beg for bread. The righteous man is one who obeys God's instructions and whenever God makes a demand of them, they obey joyfully. Remember King Solomon, when it was time for the sacrifice, just a recommended animal was enough for sacrifice but Solomon gave and gave until there was no room to put the sacrifice again. The Bible further tells us that he kept the people for seven days and fed them throughout. God was touched.

On the eighth day he sent the people away: and they blessed the king, and went unto their tents joyful and glad of heart for all the goodness that the Lord had done for David his servant, and for Israel his people.
1 Kings 8:66.

Their hearts were excited. The Bible says, when you give to the poor you are lending to the Lord. When you take care of God's agenda or people, he will surprise you.
God was touched by Solomon's sacrifice, not mere giving, but sacrifice. God was so touched that He told Solomon said ask me anything. He was pleased with such dimension of love. Love the

Lord with all thine heart, with all thine strength, for God so loved the world that He gave ... has your love gotten to a point that it moves God?

It is not the giving, it is the love with which it is done, because love will compel you to give. People are always moved to give by other factors other than their love for God. If it is not done out of love, it is not a sincere giving. This is why some prosperity preachers get at you.

They increase your appetite and stir you to give. After giving all you later realize that you gave out of flesh, not love. Come to the place of ardent love for the Father. Love God to the point where nothing hinders you. So that you can change the ugly names people and even your family members call you. Can you go all the way when God makes demand of you? When Bible says you should carry your cross, it means bearing pain and death to self for the eternal purpose of God to be fulfilled.

He that loveth father or mother more than me is not worthy of me: and he that loveth son or daughter more than me is not worthy of me.
Matthew 10:37.

Can you suffer persecution for his sake? Can you let go some things for the sake of the Kingdom? People talk about Smith Wigglesworth's miracles but they don't know that there was more to it. Study shows that he was crazy for God that he read the Bible after every 15 minutes and that if he was given food to eat, he will have to do Bible study before he eats. Because he wanted God's Kingdom to prosper, he fasted for one year and he was praying all-nights, after which strange results began in his life and ministry. It's all about sacrificial love for God's kingdom.

Bible says we should bear the reproach for the sake of Christ. What can you let go for the sake of the kingdom. Most times our comfort is our priority when God should be our priority. Can you let go your 'Isaac' for his sake? Check your prayer points, when was the last time you prayed about the advancement of God's Kingdom. Have you discovered that every time people are asked to pray for the kingdom, their morale is low but if it's personal, their morale becomes high? It tells you where the love of the people is. If we are asked to pray for souls, you will see people's prayer tempo go low.

It is not how you pray for yourself, it's not about what you do for yourself but what you do for the Kingdom. What can you suffer for the Kingdom? Some of us are ashamed of being called Christians; some cannot hold their Bible in public, they wrap it while some can't call Jesus in public, for the fear of death. Can God make a demand of your job or make a demand of your time? That is where it begins. It doesn't begin from just sowing ten percent.

Do you know why God ask you to pay tithe? God is so rich that He does not need your money or tithe, but he needs an access to influence your finance. The tithe is a test of your faith in God as my source. It is partnership with God. Our inconsistency in tithe is the reason many don't enjoy the benefit of tithing. You know why you can't give tithe and get the result immediately? It is because your consistency must be tested the same way your love must be tested. If He says give me your first fruit, don't complain. Complaining kills the life in a seed. If you will ever grumble before giving don't give because even if you finally give, it will not be of any benefit to you. In fact, don't give that money because it will not help you, seeing that the heart is not right. So if you are giving to God, do so with a cheerful heart and out of the abundance of your love for him. Money is a test of man's love for God because it is one of man's dependence for survival.

John D. Rockefeller

John D. Rockefeller was one of the richest men in the world at a point. At age 52, he was the richest. He was giving out 50% of his income to the Kingdom, kept 30% for himself and 20% of his income went for savings. He became sick at a point and was dying. So he decided to give out all that he had to the poor because he didn't want to die having his wealth in his possession. He took half out of the whole money he had and started giving it out. While he did that, he started recovering from his illness. Doctors had said he will die within a year but as the year went by, the man became stronger and died after 40 years. He died at 92 years because God preserved him on the account of his love for Him and His people which he proved by his selfless giving.

It doesn't matter the economic meltdown of America, it will come up. America will always control the World economy. It is not a matter of whether there is a melt down or not. I will tell you why. The constitution of America was written by 300 people and only two among those people were not born again. They agreed in the constitution that only 85% of the people's income should be taxable. The government only taxed them from the 85% because as a Christian Senate, they said we will not tax the 15% so that 10% can go for tithe and 5% for offering. So, they only placed tax on 85% of the income of citizens. That was what raised America to the height she got to. The ones that were not born again understood the pattern and gave as well.

> *But the liberal deviseth liberal things; and by liberal things shall he stand.*
> *Isaiah 32:8.*

The liberal man scattereth but he that holdeth tendeth to poverty. So, God will surely test you. Your love and sacrifice preserves you from your enemies. It also positions you for greatness. How much can you let go for the Kingdom? That is how to serve God. Can you love God so much that you don't have to be cajoled, to come to church to be blessed? There is something called the sacrifice of fellowship. The Bible says don't forsake the gathering… sometimes coming to church can be a sacrifice. Even when your body feels like being alone, insist that you must come. When you are dead in God, you don't need any form of cajoling. No justifiable reason should keep you out of church, not because of the Pastor but because you love God. Ask yourself, how far can I go for him?.

Before you start complaining, when He makes demand of you, will you obey? Rockefeller went to be with the Lord at 92 years of age. Your service notwithstanding, God requires that your heart be right. That is why though David was a good singer, he still prayed "Lord try my heart". I know this sound like a very hard prayer but it's a prayer you need to pray for yourself, that you will not live your life in futility. How much can you gather to become rich? Since you know that it is not about you but him, don't see his instructions as burdensome. A church that loves God doesn't need a preacher to stir it to give. I don't support preachers who just preach to stir members to give because of their personal interest. Any giving that is initiated by pressure from a message is of the flesh.

That is why for some people there is nothing you can do, to make them prosper. Bible says "... it is He that giveth thee power to make wealth..." he can only bless those whose hearts are right. It means you have to be aligned to him to receive the prosperity of the kingdom. No anointing oil or word can enrich you, instead, when you have a wrong heart. It is all about the heart. A man that will be great will be known from the way he handles the things of God. If it was not given by him, it cannot be preserved by him. Anytime you complain and decline in faithfulness in paying your tithe it shows that your heart has not been perfected in God, if it has been, no pressure will hinder you from paying your tithe.

Do you know God pays close attention during tithes and offering? Jesus sat where the people were giving offering and the Bible says he was observing. He is very much interested in what you give to him and how you give to him. He was not identifying who gave but he watched how they gave. He commended the widow who gave her last. She had a justifiable reason not to give but she still gave her all.

The woman of Zeraphat explained to the prophet her predicament – small flour and two sticks was what she and her son had to eat and die, but Elijah said, make for me first. God doesn't place a demand on you out of wickedness but because your obedience is the platform upon which his blessings rest. Your poverty therefore, should not be a barrier. God makes demand from someone who doesn't have to create a channel to bless him. If you have to suffer for the Kingdom, will you do it joyfully? Some people at such times will ask if it is their minds or the Spirit of God leading them. You can't mistakenly give to God.

If you realize your poverty is lasting too long, check, probably there was a demand of God upon you that you did nothing about. God brought out the children of Israel out of Egypt with gold and silver and still asked them for that gold and silver for the building of His temple. The foolish among them will hold back, but the wise will know that this will bring the source of their provision to dwell among them and establish His covenant with them. God sometimes positions you for a blessing by placing a demand on you.

Honour The Prophet Over Your Life

Another factor or access into Kingdom wealth is having a priest who speaks over your life and declares the word of the Lord into your spirit; that brings light and empowerment to you. A true priest is one entrusted by God to ensure you stay under God's will, covering and blessing. God commands His priests on how to bless His people.

Speak unto Aaron and unto his sons, saying, On this wise ye shall bless the children of Israel, saying unto them; The Lord bless thee, and keep thee: The Lord make his face shine upon thee, and be gracious unto thee: The Lord lift up his countenance upon thee, and give thee peace.
Numbers 6:23-26.

Because the Lord wants to prosper you, the prophecy of God's priest over your life cannot be undermined (Ezra 6:14). Besides being an ardent lover of God, you need a priest or prophet who will speak into and over your life and in most cases refers to your pastor under whom you are nourished spiritual. I don't mean busybody lazy pastor who suck life out of members: Always preaching money for personal greed.

Trust not Uncertain Riches

The wealth of this world creates a false sense of security. When the money is in the bank account, you feel happy and when it is not, you are scared. That sense of instability and lack of confidence you show means that your confidence is in certain riches.

Lay not up for yourselves treasures in earth, where moth and rust doth corrupt, and where thieves break through and steal: But lay not up for yourselves treasures in Heaven, where neither moth nor rust doth corrupt, and where thieves break through and steal.
Matthew6:19-20.

THE GREAT APOSTLE (BABALOLA)

The field of mysticisms and spiritual phenomena are beginning to attract the attention and loving interest of the modern age. In hunger and persistent search for reality, answers to many unanswered question of which have transcended beyond what meets the eyes and what bare hands could handle. This hunger and interest to understand spiritual things, to unearth deep mysteries of the unseen realm, and most importantly to know and intercourse with divinity has driven you to reading this book, of which I'm assured by the intensity of the spirit will not leave you frustrated. In order to understand the varied moves, manifestations and waves of God, it is essential to study the character of the founding personalities. In other words, to understand a particular fact of revival expression and phenomenon, it is essential to also visit the lives of those men and women who are genius of revival.They were men who walked in fearful dimension of Gods power.

   On this basis, we'll look at the life of one of the notable figures of the Alaadura movement Joseph Ayo Babalola, a man that has been acclaimed "the central and the most notable figure in the whole Alaadura movement. Knowing that many revivals have come and gone and we talk about the exploits of those revivalists, this study is proposed to ignite a fire in us, to cause a craving in our spirit for the raw power of God and to instill a desperate hunger to carry on from where they (past revivalists) stopped to greater feats. Knowing that the later glory should be greater than the former.

Overview

Apostle Babalola: a man filled with wisdom and founder of Christ Apostolic Church (CAC). Quiet but eloquent, courageous and hardworking, the great general who possessed a super human physique, beautiful straight hair, eyes that could see further than the human eye even into the invisible, loud resounding voice, resilient body that could go for days without food or water, unusual strength, filled with the Joy of the Lord, a music lover, song writer, husband to Dorcas Adetoun, father of five, mentor to so many and father of many.

   His Birth

According to parental testimony, the birth of Babalola was preceded by an unusual and unexplainable incidents; the same heavily characterized his entire life. Three months to his birth, Madam Martha Rotimi his mother contracted small pox; she was then relocated to a farm in IGBO NIYUN FOREST for treatment. One day during the dry season while Joseph's father was in his farm, something strange happened. Someone set fire on the bush leading to those (bushes) surrounding the hut where Joseph's father and mother were staying. At the sight of this, David

(Joseph's father) lamented: "we are in trouble, we did not die of small pox epidemic in the town but we will now perish through this strange fire" meanwhile animals of different shapes and kind trying to escape, stopped within fifty feet radius away and began moving toward them (in the hut). While they waited for their dramatic end, without any external effort, the fire suddenly went down until it finally quenched, then the animals all went their ways the other. On the 25th of April, 1904, the sound of a mighty thunder which was followed by a suspicious shaking accompanied the birth of Babalola to the family of Mr. / Mrs. David Rotimi of the Anglican Church in the community of ODO-OWA in IIOFA, Kwara state (Nigeria).

Seven days later, he was named Joseph Ayo Babalola. A name that distinguished him from every other member of the family as the only child who did not bear the family name; Rotimi. At his naming ceremony, it was said that bush meat was in abundance. While growing up, Joseph would say certain things and act in certain ways that were clearly above the wisdom and imagination of one at the age of 3 as he was. One day looking intently at the sky with a loving admiration, he was noticed by his mother who asked what he was looking at and he replied "can't you see what I'm seeing? I'm looking at the king of glory" this response made his mother utterly surprised. When he was seven years old, he was offered a piece of meat that had been sacrificed to an idol by his grandmother, an item which she had brought from an idolatrous ceremony. But Babalola rejected it with a resounding rebuke to her saying "mama ye Jeboyeye" meaning (grand ma, stop eating sacrifices) this resulted in her becoming a Christian. Those are some of the first signs that proved he was not an ordinary child but a carrier of God's supernatural power.

Educational and Vocational Training

At age 14, Babalola and his uncle Mr. Moses Rotimi left Odo owe for Lagos (in 1918) with educational plans in mind. He first began his education in Awori-land but on the transfer of his uncle he was enrolled at Methodist school at Ajaje at Ebute-metta in 1921 where he completed two sessions before withdrawing again in 1924. They moved to Oshogbo that same year and after a period he again enrolled at Mes School, in the town where he read up to standard five before he finally dropped out to learn trade. Within a short time he mastered blacksmithing. But had no money to buy the equipment so he began to work at a hospital to raise money. It was during this period that the public department employed him as a roller driver and paid him 4 pounds per month. At the time Babalola joined them and they were working on Akure Ijesha road, and within a short time, he had his own workforce and began to handle jobs to the satisfaction of his European supervisor, Mr. Ferguson in 1928.

His Encounter and Call

The 25th of September, 1928 was a remarkable day in Babalola's life. The day a faithless steam roller refused to work. It started about two weeks earlier. He said "I couldn't sleep for a whole week both night and day. My spirit was rejoicing and joyous as I read my bible (Psalms 1 – 150). I did not feel sleepy neither did I fall sick." Before a person can seek God, God by his sovereign grace must arrest the attention of his wandering sheep.

On the 9th of October, I was still on the roller site, at about 12noon, we heard a mighty voice that sounded like 10,000 thunders calling my name, Joseph! Joseph!! Joseph!!! Leave this work you are doing, if you don't leave this work you are doing, this year you will be cut off from the land of the living "these happened thrice but I was only concerned with getting the roller to function. Until two days later the same event repeated itself, while amidst many people including my workers. But this time the voice said "if you don't leave this work the roller would never move again. Concerned and surprised, I shouted back "who are you calling me and which work do you have for me to do?" A lot of people asked who I was speaking to after the encounter. So I finally left the job and immediately went home. The same voice again said if I wanted to know him, I should begin a seven day fast.

At mid-night on the seventh day of the fast, the Lord appeared to me physically, and asked if I wanted to eat. I replied yes. Jesus Christ stood before me in a sparkling white garment which was touching the ground but did not say anything, and there was another being that was standing reaching the sky. He gave me half a tuber of yam to eat, which I did eat, then he said, 'with that ration, I fed the world in a certain year'. The Lord gave him (Babalola) three symbolic gifts: a hand bell, an iron and a bottle of water. These three gifts as explained to Babalola were symbolic; the bell was to call people to prayer, bring the angels of God down to his meetings and drive evil forces away. The iron staff represented the apostolic authority to subdue evil forces, while the bottle of water was given to him for the healing of all sicknesses and diseases. This commission to heal was the origin of the doctrine of divine healing in Babalola's ministry and it resulted to the inception of Christ Apostolic Church. It is important to note that Babalola came to the understanding of the doctrine of divine healing by a revelation of God.

The Quest

The seven day fast had fetched him the visitation and the assignment but not the power for the assignment. Just like the Lord told his disciples to wait in Jerusalem till they be endued with power from on high, Babalola therefore continued seeking the face of God for the power of the Holy Ghost to prosecute his apostolic commission, during this time he was divinely directed to Prophet Joseph Fapohunda of whom the hand of the Lord was upon. While he waited (fasting and praying) until he received the baptism of the Holy Spirit.

A Mad Preacher

After the baptism of the Holy Spirit, he was constantly visited by angels; they brought him visions and instructions preparing him for ministry. After the angels had given Apostle Babalola a lot of revelations, they instructed him to go to Ilofa, his hometown. He gave his entire savings (14 pounds) to the fellowship leader, Prophet Joseph Fapohunda and moved to his hometown (Odo – owo). God directed him to go and warn the people of idolatry and fetish acts. God told him to go naked covering only his private part, and put ashes on his face and body. Coincidentally Babalola entered the town on a market day when the town was full of people.

They thought among themselves that he had lost his mind. He began to preach the gospel, the entire town was moved and there was great stir and consternation as people fled when they saw him, he rang the bell round the town preaching. Many people advised his father to bind him with fetters, because to them, he had gone mad. Although, the father had no understanding of his son's new act, he rejected their suggestions. He insisted his son was normal, as there was no history of madness in his ancestry.

Babalola began to prophesy to them as he preached the gospel, telling them that evil beasts would invade the town and devour the people if they do not repent. But the people rebelled against his message. And rather seized him with force and took him to the district officer at Ilorin, for him to be arrested. Despite their efforts to detain him, the district officer released Babalola and dismissed the case. The district officer was touched by the Holy Spirit to act this way. When the people of Ilofa saw that Babalola could not be arrested in Ilorin, they sought to kill him through demonic powers, which they boasted of. They made several attempts to conjure their demonic power and charms against him but they all failed. There was a particular witch doctor, who claimed he needed just seven days but still his power failed him. As the day of the fulfillment of the prophecy of the evil beasts attack approached, they prepared resisting the beasts, to this, since they could not kill the young apostle. They sharpened their machetes and oiled their guns, getting ready to kill the beasts when they come into town.

Three days before the doom's day, the Lord told Babalola to still announce to the people that no one would be able to draw his/ her spear from its sheath or carry his/her gun when the evil beasts attack the town. The people in response to his announcement boasted of their skills and readiness for combat.

In confirmation, within fourty five days, an epidemic of small pox invaded the town. No one indeed could draw his/her sword or carry his/her gun to confront the evil beasts that infested their bodies. The word of the Lord came to pass.

At this juncture, all those who had the small pox surrendered to God by calling on the man of God and they were immediately healed. Those who were adamant and criticized him, died of the disease while others came to him for prayers and received their healing. Soon after that, a revival broke out on the Anglican Church, Babalola began to go out for early morning preaching, and open air crusades in the centre of the town. Due to persecution they were forced out of the Anglican Church. They moved to a member's house where the people received the baptism of the Holy Spirit and spoke in tongues.

Ministerial Exploits and Revival Missions

The revival missions began by bringing back to life a dead child in September, 1920. It was followed by the healing of about hundred lepers, sixty blind and fifty lame persons in three weeks. This also resulted in the desolation of churches in Illesa because their members transferred their allegiance to the revivalist; all the patients in Wesley Hospital Illesa abandoned their beds to seek healing from Babalola.

This divine kickoff of the great Revival of 1930 saw people coming from most parts of Africa and Diaspora without posters or TV adverts. In June 25th 1931, he slew the sinister Abugabu (dragon) of the jungles of yogumbo, wielding the Holy Ghost sword imbued with the fire of the Lord. Thereafter, with a bell and a Yoruba bible in his hand, he turned Yoruba land and eastern Nigeria to God, preaching repentance, renunciation of idolatry, the importance of prayer and fasting and the power of God to heal the sick. Wherever and whenever he prayed into the water for therapeutic purposes, effective healing was procured for those who drank it. Enabled by the power of the Holy Spirit; he could spend several weeks in prayer. He regularly saw angels who delivered divine messages to him. On one occasion an angel appeared in one of his prayers and forbade him to wear caps.

Babalola was invited to Illesa, so he joined the delegation of peace makers who were sent to resolve the controversy among the leaders of the faith tabernacle over doctrinal issues like the use of western and traditional drugs versus divine healing, polygamy and whether polygamous husbands should be allowed to partake of the Lord's Supper. As the reconciliatory talks were going on, suddenly a mighty sweeping revival broke out on faith tabernacle congregation at Oke-Oye, Illesa. This included raising a dead child, and healing of those afflicted with diseases. Many mighty works were performed through the use of the prayer bell and people drinking the consecrated water from a stream called Omi-Ayo (stream of Joy). As thousands were converted to the faith tabernacle, there was no space in the church hall, so revival meetings were shifted to an open field. Members claim that hopeless barren women were made fruitful, women who had been carrying their pregnancies for long years were wonderfully delivered, the dumb spoke, lunatic were cured, witches confessed and demon possessed were exorcised.

A revelation was later given to Babalola to burn down a big tree in front of the Oba's palace. The big tree was believed traditionally, to be the rendezvous of witches and wizards. The juju tree was greatly feared and sacrifices were usually made to the spirits believed to reside in it. There were apprehensions that this bold act would result to his instant death, since it was expected to arouse the anger of the gods. But amazingly, the prophet did not die, rather he grew stronger in the Lord. That single event made seven of the Oba of Illesa, the most important people in the town to fear and respect the prophet.

The wave of this revival spread from Illesa to Ibadan, Ijebu, Lagos Efon Alaaye, Aramoko, Ekiti and Abeokuta. No greater revival preceded that of Babalola. The prophet was directed by the Holy Spirit to go out on further missionary journeys accompanied by some of his disciples. He went to Offa (Kwara State), people turned out to hear his preaching and receive miracles.

The Muslims became jealous and for that reason, incited the community against him. Traditionally, the place was a forbidden forest but he established his prayer ground there and when no harm came upon them, the inhabitants were inspired to accept the new faith.

The success of the revival was accelerated by the conversion of the Oba of Efon and Oba of Aramoko in 1932, after being released from jail he was entreated to come to Calabar by Mr. Cyprian. The prophet sought God's direction and he had success. Certain members of a national church in Duke town received the gift of the Holy Spirit. When he returned and settled for a while, in 1935 he married Dorcas and the following year went to the Gold coast.

Problems and Challenges Faced by Babalola

Ayo Babalola was sent out of the Anglican church of his village by his Bishop because most members of the church saw visions, spoke in tongues and prayed vigorously. When he deduced that this behavior was caused by a swamp witch, he went into her hut where she quickly turned into a terrible bird beast. He tricked the bird-witch into eating gogundo berries from his hand allowing him to clonk her on the head and broke the curse. This led to his joining the faith Tabernacle church in November, 1929. After the revival, he retreated to his home to fortify himself spiritually.

While there, a warrant for his arrest for preaching against witches and some of their evil practices was issued and he was sentenced to six months in Benin City in March, 1932.

The spectacular evangelism brought with it a wave of persecution to all who rushed into the new faith. The mission churches became jealous and hostile. The Nigerian Faith Tabernacle was ceded to the British Apostolic Church, consequently the name changed to Apostolic Church. Doctrinal differences began to appear, the white missionaries were found using quinine and other tablets.

The controversy could not be resolved as a result, the group split. One fraction of the church made Oko-oye its base and retained the name Apostolic Church. The other larger fraction in which Babalola was a leader became Christ Apostolic Church.

His Death

He died at age 55 on the 26th of July, 1959 as a result of illness. On the 24th he returned to Ibadan to attend the general council meeting slated for that day and on 25th, after conducting prayers for ministers and others, he sent for Bayo Adeyinka at Ede to prepare him a place to sleep. When he arrived, he requested to be allowed to have some sleep, as he had not slept for nine days due to the series of meetings.

He woke up three hours later and took some tea and slept again at 6 O'clock later on Bayo went to his room and he began to talk to him about a great convention which will soon be held at his home town, he was speaking in parable. He also sent for a prophet called Babajide and began narrating how he started ministry, then he bid everyone farewell after which, he took a nap. When he woke up he returned Bayo's covering cloth to him and he was asked why? He said "A man should sleep with his own clothes" Around 5pm, he breathed heavily three (3) times and the vibration shook the entire building before he exiled from the world. His personal attendants rushed to call Bayo Yinka and the church leaders; who started praying for his restoration. But the prayer was on, when Bayo spiritually saw that the heavenly host had come to meet the prophet and joyfully admitted him into glory.

Babalola had laid down his sword at Jesus' feet so he could not return to earth again. That same night, his corpse was arranged to be taken to Efon-Alaaya. J.A. Babalola contacted power from God through the price of consecration; of prayer and fasting, of obedience, of separation, of commitment and of self-denial.

Refrences:

1. en.wikipedia.org\wiki\joseph ayo babalola
2. www.dacb.org\..\babalola2_joseph.html

ST. JOSEPH OF CUPERTINO

St. Joseph was mystically born on 17 June, 1603. His father died before he was born, leaving debts he has incurred, and as a result, the creditors drove his mother, Francesca Panara from her home and she was obliged to give birth to her child in a stable. Joseph had an ecstatic vision while at school and this was renewed several times. Joseph was able to read but poorly. Yet infused by knowledge and supernatural light, he not only surpassed ordinary men in learning of the schools but could solve the most intricate questions.

Life and Ministry

In March 1628 Joseph became a priest at 25years of age despite his limitations and opinion of men. Joseph was often not allowed to attend choir, go to common refectory, walk in procession or say mass in church but was ordered to remain in his room. Evil minded and envious men even brought him before the inquisition and he was sent from one lonely house of the Capuchins or Franciscas to another but Joseph retained his joyous spirit, submitting confidently to divine providence. He faced lots of persecution from men in the monastery. Joseph practiced mortification and fasting to such a degree that he kept seven Lents of forty days each year and during many of them tasted no food except on Thursdays and Sundays.

Ecstatic Flights and Manifestations

Joseph spent long hours alone in his room in deep meditation and was often found wandering about as if in a daze. On some occasions the friars found him in different places such as the chapel of St. Barbara but Joseph was unaware of how he had come to these places. This was the Lord preparing him for special missions by giving him the gift of ecstatic flight. In October 4, 1630 the town's people of Cupertino held a procession in honour of St. Francis of Assisi. Joseph was assisting in the procession when suddenly he soared into the air and remained there motionless before the crowd. When he eventually came down, he was so embarrassed that he fled to his mother's house to hide from the crowd. This experience earned him the name "the flying saint."

On one Christmas evening when Joseph heard the music of some shepherds who had come to join him in celebrating the birth of Christ, he began to dance and sing with joy and was lifted up like a bird to the high altar. He remained there for about fifteen minutes without disturbing the candles or burning his cloths. On another occasion, during the celebration in honour of St. Francis, Joseph rose above the pulpit and remained there for some time with his arm outstretched and knees bent. On several occasions, Joseph would be lifted up in the air and would come down when his superiors commanded him.

His Secret

Joseph practiced the most severe forms of mortification. He scourged himself for hours, which often caused bleeding, He refused to eat bread, meat or to drink wine and lived only on fruits and herbs. This led to the deterioration of his health and often left him on the point of collapse. Joseph's life began to change considerably by the amount of spiritual exercises he engaged in.

His ecstasies (Elevations) were becoming more numerous and frequent. On hearing the name of Jesus and Mary he would go into ecstasy and remain there for some time until the superior commanded him under heavy obedience to return to his senses.

He became famous for his ecstasies, and gifts of levitation. He began to attract so many pilgrims to the monastery that his superior had to transfer him from one monastery to another to avoid the commotion. Those flights were so astonishing that there was hardly any other saint known to have received such a super-abundant gift from God.

His Trial

Joseph was greatly disturbed over these incidents and wished to withdraw from public eye. Although he considered it a cross he must bear he nevertheless asked his superior if he could say mass privately as he feared that people were watching him intensely to see if he would make any mistake that could be reported. Because these visions were so extraordinary, father Joseph's virtue was also tested. God himself permitted Joseph to be severely tempted by the devil. Added to this, he suffered for many years from dryness of heart. But all these trials could not embitter his heart, he placed it within the wound of the saviour's side and preserved peace of mind. He had no other wish but to do the will of God. All of Joseph's experiences brought many accusers to him. He was summoned to Rome for trial by the minister general in Rome. He was sentenced to the friary at the tomb of St. Frances of Assisi (also known as the sacred comere) in Assisi. This brought great joy to him who had always dreamt of living in Assisi near the tomb of his seraphic fathers. This trial brought joy to Joseph and he concluded that this was God's plan.

He was to be tested by the withdrawal of consolation, by persecutions, temptations and spiritual dryness which were meant to purify his soul. Joseph experienced "dark night of his soul." He no longer had ecstasies or experienced aridity during spiritual reading, while praying and even celebrating mass. God seemed deaf to his pleading and he slumped into a depression far greater than he had experienced before at Grottella. The devil frequently tempted Joseph with a great load. The devil frequently tempted Joseph in many ways which caused him to wake from night mares. These assaults lasted almost two years but Joseph, though terrified, was able to resist and his soul was to become even firmer and stronger and unshakable. God's supernatural grace had not allowed him to be tasted beyond his limits. He would often remark "it is better to consider giving up everything in this world for God's glory, for it adds to our merit when we suffer for his divine majesty." To suffer for the love of God is a greater blessing and man is not worthy of it. These trials strengthened him and at Assisi many people came to him for prayers and advices including the Bishop, Monsignor Baglioni malatesta.

Miracles of St. Joseph

St. Joseph lived in Assisi and spent his entire day in prayer and hours of meditations. When celebrating mass, he would often levitate. He found it difficult to break bread when he perceives that someone is living in serious sin. During his trial preparation, he requested the "statue of the cross" to be placed along the road leading to the Grottela Church. Ten men tried to place the last cross in place but they could not lift it up. Joseph, went into ecstasy, flew up and lifted it like a piece of wood into place. At one time, he was in danger of being struck by a severe storm but through his prayers the hurricane ceased. On another occasion, through Joseph's intercession, a doctor was able to pass by without being noticed by assassins who sought to attack and rob him on his way home to Assisi. At another time the minister general of the order was saved from drowning when he sought the intercession of St. Joseph. St. Joseph told the minister general how he saw him in danger from his fall just as he was saying mass and how he prayed for his safety.

Joseph was able to appear in more than one place at the same time. On one occasion, while he was still in Assisi he was seen in the little church in Grotella, where he went into ecstasy and disappeared. Another episode recalls that an old priest, who used to be Joseph's confessor, was very ill. He saw Joseph appear by the foot of his bed and reassure him that he will get well. At another time, Joseph's mother, Frances was dying and she called upon her son for help. The people present in the room noticed rays of lightening shining through the window and Frances seemed to be talking to someone, she then died whispering. "Oh Joseph my son!" Joseph saw things before they happened. On one occasion, a woman asked him to pray for her two sons who were about to receive a doctorate degree, he saw that they will soon be in heaven. Few days later they died. Through visions from God, Joseph would set out for a journey he didn't know where he was going. During one of the journeys in one of the houses, a mason who had been lame for many years was healed by Joseph.

What Kept Him

St. Joseph had a burning love for God. He committed himself to much fasting and spiritual exercises which affected his health but never caused him to relent. He was often found praying at the grave of St. Francis till midnight. Joseph's sense of obedience prevailed and he said,

I look only for the will of God.